PENGUIN BOOKS

IRELAND'S PUBS

Sybil Taylor is a freelance writer and film publicist. A former actress, she has had a varied career in publishing, public relations, and journalism, and even drove a horse carriage in Central Park for a time. She came to the United States as a very young child, a refugee from Hitler's Germany; she has been an inveterate traveler all her life. In researching this book, she discovered an Irish branch of her family that she never knew existed.

IRELAND'S PUBS

SYBIL TAYLOR

PENGUIN BOOKS

Penguin Books Ltd, Harmondsworth,
Middlesex, England
Penguin Books, 625 Madison Avenue,
New York, New York 10022, U.S.A.
Penguin Books Australia Ltd, Ringwood,
Victoria, Australia
Penguin Books Canada Limited, 2801 John Street,
Markham, Ontario, Canada L3R 1B4
Penguin Books (N.Z.) Ltd, 182–190 Wairau Road,
Auckland 10, New Zealand

First published 1983

LIBRARY OF CONGRESS CATALOGING IN PUBLICATION DATA
Taylor, Sybil.
Ireland's pubs.
Includes index.
1. Hotels, taverns, etc.—Ireland—Directories.
2. Hotels, taverns, etc.—Northern Ireland—
Directories I. Title.
TX910.I7T38   1983   647'.95415   82-15074
ISBN 0 14 00.6488 5

Printed in the United States of America by
R. R. Donnelley & Sons Company, Harrisonburg, Virginia
Set in Linotron Goudy

Photographs by Mark Fiennes and by Bord Failte—Irish Tourist Board
Maps by Paul J. Pugliese, GCI
Designed by Ann Gold

The author would like to thank Richard Barkle of Pan Am
and William Maxwell of Aer Lingus for their help and cooperation.

Pages 255–256 constitute an extension of the copyright page.

For Erika—lovely companion, shining daughter

For J.P.D.—Irish guide and muse

For William Rossa Cole—a model of restraint as I
carted away most of his Irish library

For Richard Brown—whose fault this book is

For Scott—"longtime sunshine"

For my fellow travelers
SLAINTE!

CONTENTS

There is magic about the country
in some of her moods
which runs through the fingers
like water as one tries to lay
hold of it.

—Honor Tracy

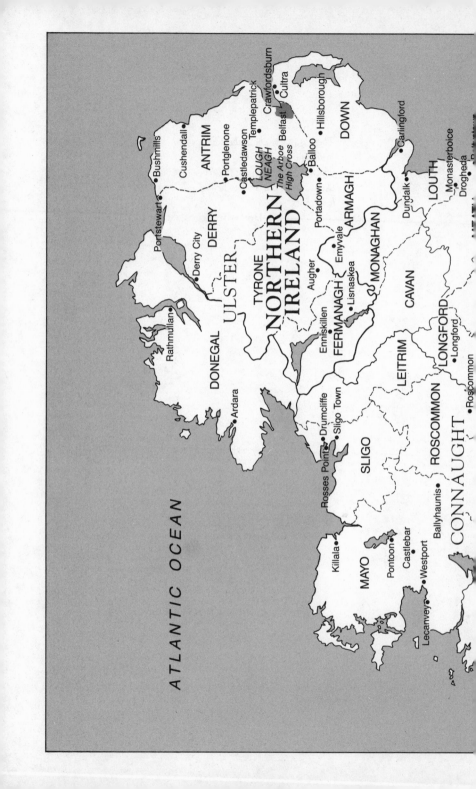

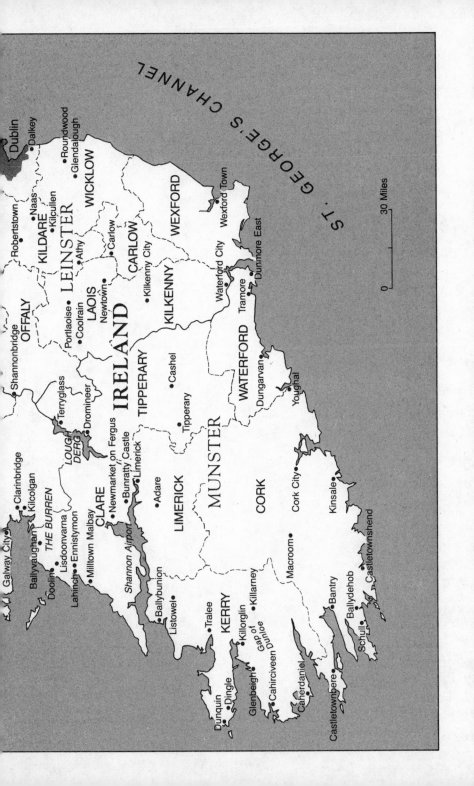

PREFACE: AN UNASHAMED APOLOGY

In Ireland the inevitable never happens, the unexpected always.
—J. P. Mahaffy

Ireland is so faceted and so paradoxical a place that I cannot claim the ability to encompass its complex history or the power to evoke its mercurial people and landscape. All I hope to do is give a mosaic of impressions and facts that taken together form an introductory picture of the country, and to provide a guide to some of Ireland's pubs as the best means of exploration.

I'm sure I've missed a few good ones and can well imagine the humorous Irish disdain that will greet some of my omissions. I may also have included the odd pub that is no longer up to its former standards or simply is no longer. Things change slowly in Ireland . . . still, they change.

So please forgive me in advance . . . there are 11,000 pubs in Ireland and I'm still researching.

God bless, as they say, and raise one for me if you like the place I've brought you to.

THE PUBLIC HOUSE
IN IRELAND

A pint of plain is your only man.
　　　　　—Flann O'Brien, *At Swim-Two-Birds*

Hours: Weekdays: 10:30 a.m. to 2:30 p.m.; 3:30 to 11:00 p.m. (11:30 summers). Sunday: 12:30 to 2:00 p.m.; 4:00 to 10:00 p.m. Outside the urban areas the pubs remain open between 2:30 and 3:30. The lunchtime break is irreverently referred to as the "Holy Hour." (See p. 220 for hours in Northern Ireland.)

Food: Most pubs, even if they are not also restaurants, will serve "pub grub": salads, sandwiches, cold platters, soups. The quality of the pub grub varies from pub to pub. Pub grub and food are listed when they are a particular feature. Note: Phone numbers have not been listed, since you will not need to call ahead in most cases. In addition, the Irish phone system is to be avoided whenever possible.

Officially and politically, Dublin and Belfast are Ireland's capitals, but the true center of Irish life for centuries has been her pubs. In a sparsely populated country (3½ million for the Irish Republic plus 1½ million for Northern Ireland), the pub has served many functions; grocery store, funeral parlor, concert hall, restaurant, bar, political forum, congenial meeting place, courting corner, and, most of all, a place for talk.

Nowhere is the word more revered than in Ireland and nowhere is it used with such expertise and with such a sense of delight as in an Irish pub. To listen to talk in a 200-year-old pub is to be part of a living tradition—and have fun at the same time.

15

Though an unfortunate and misguided flurry of "modernization" in the 1950s and '60s has in many cases replaced the intricate tiled floors with carpeting and the venerable wooden tables with Formica, old-style pubs can still be found in both urban and rural areas.

Recently, there have been pubs remodeled for comfort without demolishing the original ambience. Perhaps this is a sign of Ireland's developing sense of the value of national tradition.

Pubs are so integral to Irish life that it is calculated there is one pub for every fifty people; although at 5:00 p.m. in Dublin, it can feel as though all Ireland is crowded into the pub you're in, with everyone competing for the Oscar Wilde Award for Wit.

In the country, pubs are often a focal point of the village, serving double duty as grocery store or post office. Sometimes you don't even know you're in a pub until you hear a murmur of voices, glance through a doorway, and note the peaceful consumption of pints going on in a dim back room. Such pubs usually have just the name of the proprietor over the door, and a little store in front with windows piled with canned goods, sneakers, headache powders, gardening tools, bananas, oranges, and tomatoes. (Try the tomatoes—small, sweet, juicy, delicious.)

Other pubs can be easily recognized by their elaborate and wonderfully imaginative façades painted in brightly colored, geometric patterns, black-and-white designs, or *trompe l'oeil* styles cleverly reproducing cut stone.

You'll also encounter storefronts with lace-curtained windows discreetly hiding the leisurely drinkers inside from prying or unfriendly eyes.

Pub exteriors can be works of art to delight the discerning eye, with imaginatively lettered signs, doors a frosty fantasy of beveled and curlicued glass, and ornate embellishments of carved wood.

The interiors, too, range from the humble to the grandiose, from the cozy to the palatial. Old-time public houses in towns are partitioned into "snugs," wood-walled compartments that create the perfect smoky atmosphere for private talk and drink. It is no wonder that much revolutionary conspiring took place in pubs, as well as clandestine meetings of all sorts. You also will find the snug conducive to the exchange of confidences, so consider yourself warned if you've got secrets you wish to keep inviolate.

Many old pubs will have a first compartment with a low, wide counter; behind it is a wall lined with ancient little wooden drawers. This is a relic of the old days when tea, spices, and herbs were sold in the front part and drinking was confined to the back. As you move into the deeper regions of the room, the age-darkened bar unfolds either into an intricate series of partitioned spaces or as a long marble-topped altar behind which the barman officiates, sometimes with his assistants, the whole a repository of storied memory and flashes of inspiration.

A good barman does much to inspire his customers. To see a publican dispensing spirits to an eager crowd is to witness a feat of agility and competence. He works with incredible speed, a friendly smile, and a genial quip, against a jumbled background of bottles, glasses, mirrors, ornaments, and gewgaws, all housed in a wooden framework that sometimes resembles the elaborate carved headboard of a bed of state.

A good Dublin barman is a font of information, story, and jest, a diplomat, and a shrewd judge of people. He is a canny businessman with the physical dexterity and memory to serve 200 people well-pulled pints while remembering names and personal quirks.

Once a city pub has a reputation for serving a good pint, the discriminating drinker will frequent it, arriving with friends to discuss the merits of this particular pint compared with the one down the road.

Pulling a Good Pint: The secret of pulling Guinness is to pour the pint slowly, let it settle, and then fill the glass up to make sure the head forms properly. There's a technique to watching the "mushroom" come up, building up the head in the glass, leveling it out, topping it off, and leveling it out once more.

With a properly poured pint, the quaffer should be able to drink the whole glass through the foam of the head, the same principle operating as with Irish coffee, where you drink the coffee through the cream on top.

If you ask an Irish barman, he'll draw a shamrock for you in the thick foam on the head. You should be able to make out the shape of it in the dregs of the pint when you've finished drinking.

A lot of the skill involved in pulling the perfect pint is instinctive and unconscious; the barman must have an eye for the way the beer behaves, a feeling for the treatment of it. He studies the beer as it rises in the glass and listens to his customer's comments. His care for his taps and his lines, and his understanding of his product, create a classic drink—dark, smooth, and satisfying.

The writer Danny Costello, with classic Irish ability to capture the telling detail, gives a fine dissertation on "froth" in the magazine *The Bell*.

A Note on Froth: Generation and Disposal of. Putting a top or a "Roman collar" on stout is not as simple as it looks. It must be done swiftly and expertly, employing the minimum of ancillary vessels and sleight-of-hand. The actual drinking is nothing if not individual and publicans can read soiled glasses as a Scotland Yard detective reads fingerprints. Two friends may have identical pints of draught placed before them, the one disposes of his froth in the first mouthful and has a tolerably clean glass afterwards; the other nurses his froth to the bottom and leaves rings on his glass after every mouthful. When a pint glass is filled, the surplus froth is removed with a ruler or by a time-hallowed if unhygienic breath. The most characteristic pose of the small-town publican is with his mouth punch over an overflowing pint measure, a cheffish cock to his head and his cheeks dilated. The lips are dry since there is no anticipatory saliva. When used for topping pints, whalebone is believed to impart a virtue to the drink.

It is the publican who creates the mood and flavor of a pub and therefore draws to his establishment a clientele in sympathy with his particular personality. The majority of habitués have their favorite haunts and rarely take their patronage elsewhere. Those who do move from pub to pub often have interesting reasons: one man who doesn't appear at the same place on consecutive evenings, fearing a reputation as a steady drinker, travels a round of pubs that brings him full circle every ten days; another man fits the pub to his mood.

Of course country pubs have none of the crowding and clamor of city establishments. The old-fashioned watering place is usually small, the furniture worn, the tone brown, with gleams of gold where a shaft of light beams through a window. There always seem to be three or four men in caps sitting peacefully over pints and cigarettes. Billiard tables, dartboards, and TV sets are ubiquitous. In a small-town pub the personality of the owner is even more important than in the city, as Danny Costello reveals in this perfect piece called "The Small-Town Pub" (also taken from *The Bell*):

Your typical successful small-town publican is a character in his own right. Rarely reckoned a business sycophant, he is subject to a pleasing but unpredictable variety of moods, the anticipation and subsequent discussion of which provide his customers with ample food for conversation. His facial mannerisms have long since become public property, his sayings are inserted in the book of local proverbs, and the more successful he is in business, the more he is subject to mimicry. His customers demand that he be possessed of a conversational forte; a shrewd observer even on his first appearance in a small-town pub can, from various insignificant clues, deduce what subject the proprietor is strongest in. Such topics as cage-birds, coins, football, fishing, fox-terriers, contagious abortion in cattle and the overhand stroke. One of the most intelligent publicans I know believes in making his customers pull their conversational weight by the following innocent device. Once a month or so he places in a not too prominent position in the bar an example of such local produce as is in season, say a large turnip or a large mushroom or a freak potato or a bunch of heather, a hundred of scallops or even a humble sod of turf. It is amazing how these simple articles, removed from their natural habitat, assume a novel importance in the ordinary man's mind. The sod of turf could have come from any of the local bogs and to see a group of countrymen weighing the sod in their palms and examining its texture carefully before giving their opinion as to its place of origin, with the smiling, patient publican holding the secret closely, is to be given a sharp and wholesome lesson in something akin to stagecraft.

The publican, too, is expected to have the first of all local news and to give it a highly individual interpretation. He must attend the funerals of obscure hill-people, especially those having sons whose tipplings have already given token of sound alcoholic promise. His customers have long since learned to read his face as they would the country paper, and, to the initiated, his moods may be determined by such things as the way he dilates his nostrils or clanks his false teeth. One publican of my acquaintance is "good for a touch" if he is humming "Barbara Allen"; that he is in vile humour and stone deaf to all blandishments is evidenced by his whistling that popular ditty of another day, "Somewhere in Sahara."

Not that all pub life is quaint and filled with Irishmen telling yarns: there is another side to the story. The most conservative estimate of the cost of alcohol-related problems to industry in Ireland would be on the order of $12 million a year. That's a lot of jobs, or exports, or investments. Records show that alcohol plays a part in over 50 percent of all automobile collisions. With rising prosperity in Ireland came government concern and efforts to deal with these problems. With the enactment of the Breathalyzer Law, anyone who, three hours after being caught, has 100 milligrams of alcohol per 100 milliliters of blood is subject to a fine or imprisonment. The Irish media are publicizing the government's action.

A friend of mine from Belfast believes that almost every Irish family has been touched in some way by alcoholism. "Take myself," he says; "grandfather a talented painter—alcoholic; father a teacher—alcoholic." He pauses, remembering what these words mean in terms of human suffering. "The bottle stops here," he adds, pointing to himself.

The reasons for this Irish susceptibility to alcohol are open to speculation. Is it genetic? Is it caused by the sexual and societal repression embedded in the Irish heritage? Is it custom, the echo of Gaelic chieftains whose word for their brew was "usquebaugh" (from which we get "whiskey") and which translates as "water of life"?

In any case, despite the problems it causes, alcohol is still the water of life to most people in Ireland: it's a medium of exchange, a ritual, a lubricant for talk, a tranquilizer, an inspiration. Ireland is still the country where a "blonde in black" refers not only to a beautiful woman but to a pint of Guinness.

ON PUB DEPORTMENT

On entering a pub in Ireland you may think that no one is taking the slightest notice of you. As the Irish would say, "Go way outa that," or "Forget it." Even in a Dublin pub that is "chockablock," the infinitely sensitive social radar that is the heritage of the Irish is alerted: you are being scanned.

The Irish people are nothing if not polite and friendly. They will make you feel welcome and comfortable, but all in due time, and certainly not if you are aggressive. Particularly in a country pub, it's good form to settle in a while and get the drift of the talk (weather, fishing, politics). Then you can offer someone a "jar" (though it's not necessary) as a prelude to joining in the conversation. Be prepared, however, for an immediate return of the alcoholic compliment. It is traditional pub etiquette to answer a drink with a drink.

A woman by herself can have a hard time of it in the country but will be emphatically welcome in most city pubs. The majority of pubs in the city will now allow women to drink at the bar, while country pubs are still more apt to require ladies to sit in the booths, snugs, or adjoining room referred to as the "Lounge."

In some country pubs, for centuries the exclusive domain of the men of the area, all will fall silent at the entrance of strangers. Perhaps this has a historical base in the need for secrecy and reserve during times of persecution. An interesting hangover from the days of secret meetings and an example of the Irish penchant for the conspiratorial is the bartender's habit of referring to customers by their initials. "Hello, Mr. D.," says he in discreet tones, "Mr. H. was in and said not to mention anything about Mr. S. to Mr. T."

In any event, if you encounter a wall of silence and veiled glances, just order a pint and sit patiently. After a while the talk will probably resume and you might even find an appropriate moment to win a place in the conversation.

The response in a country pub is not always so taciturn. A single woman can find herself surrounded by a coterie of eager, jesting males—she will be a novelty of almost comic proportions, and the men will be quick to tease and test—each other, as well as the lady.

Teasing and testing go on in the city as well, in a more formal way: women should be prepared for what is known as the "Irish lep." This is not a shortened version of "leprechaun" but a form of brief, intense courtship crowned with a swift pounce-and-grapple. The "lepee" is free to go on with it or to laugh it all away, as laughter is the universal oil for any type of troubled Irish water.

The most prized gift in all Irish pubs, especially those of Dublin, is the ability to spin a yarn colorfully, to banter wittily, to get off the speedy rejoinder, to mesmerize your audience with the flow and style of your jokes—a good joke well told will earn you an immediate place in an Irish heart. However, it still remains the better part of valor to creep up on your joke-telling gradually, or you may find too late that *you* are the joke. Don't despair should you be a better listener than performer; your talent is doubly appreciated.

Also highly prized is the ability to understand the mysteries of Guinness. The pulling of a pint is considered an art and the quaffing thereof tantamount to a ritual. After a few expertly pulled pints, you will probably end up a convert yourself.

MUSIC, TRADITION, AND PUBS

Heavenly King, if I'd only the fingers
You gave to the piper to strike up a tune,
We'd all leave the farm
And go singing and dancing
from morning to noon.

—Anonymous

It is no accident that the Irish passport is stamped with a harp: Ireland is and always has been identified with music.

In ancient times, music and song were Ireland's vehicles for communicating the news, mythic, tragic, humorous, gossipy, romantic. So accomplished were Irish musicians that their literary/bardic art was held in high esteem in foreign lands, and flourished in the monastic seats of learning from the sixth to the twelfth centuries. To the wandering bards and their patrons, poetry and music, piping and fiddling, flute playing, singing and dancing were the stuff of life.

Traditional Irish music (or "trad") falls into two categories: the kind that is sung and the kind that makes you want to get up and jig. The songs sung in Irish are the real oldies, mythic tales or love stories of a haunting and peculiar beauty. The old ballads in English come from Scotland and England. And, of course, there are the rebel songs of the time of the Troubles.

The dancing music (I defy anyone not to tap a foot or clap) consists of jigs, reels, and hornpipes.

Through the centuries there have been thousands of itinerant musicians of various kinds, ranging from harpists (many of whom were

blind) to fiddlers, to dance masters, to those who sang and sold ballads.

At one time, the traveling poets were so numerous that Irish literature tells of wandering bards descending in force and demanding hospitality of the gentry. A legend has it that six hundred such folk,
complete with wives, servants, and a hundred hounds arrived at the
castle of King Guaire of Connaught and requested, among other things,
that they be given cuckoos to sing to them between Big and Small
Christmas. This apparently was the last straw, and only the pleas of St.
Colmcille prevented their total banishment from the country.

In medieval Ireland, and probably before, a place of honor was given
to the harp. Harpers performed the important function of accompanying oral recitations of complex systems of law, medicine, history, and
poetry: but equally important, they were artists revered for their capacity to evoke intense emotion. All of Ireland's heroes, both legendary
and historical, were skilled with the harp.

One of the most celebrated of Ireland's harpists is Turlough O'Carolan (1670–1738). His music is still performed and marveled at today,
revived by the inspired Sean O'Riada. In keeping with nomadic-poetic-
musical tradition, from Homer to the early blues singers of the American South, O'Carolan was blind, which probably had a lot to do with
his amazing memory. In *A Book of Ireland*, edited by Frank O'Connor,
Oliver Goldsmith is quoted:

> Being once at the house of an Irish nobleman where there was a musician
> present who was eminent in the profession, Carolan immediately chal-
> lenged him to a trial of skill. To carry the jest forward, his lordship per-
> suaded the musician to accept the challenge, and he accordingly played
> over on his fiddle the fifth concerto of Vivaldi. Carolan, immediately tak-
> ing his harp, played over the whole piece after him, without missing a
> note, though he had never heard it before; which produced some surprise:
> but their astonishment increased when he assured them he could make a
> concerto in the same taste himself, which he instantly composed, and
> that with such spirit and elegance that it may compare (for we have it
> still) with the finest compositions of Italy.

Traditional Irish music is enjoying a great revival, and interest is not
limited to the natives of the Emerald Isle: aficionados from all over the

world stream to Ireland in the summer and early fall to attend the many marvelous music festivals, particularly the big one in Lisdoonvarna, and the more homey one in Milltown Malbay (check with the Irish Tourist Board for dates and places).

Since Irish music and singing are still so important in Irish life, the best place to catch it "live" remains the informal and vibrant setting of a pub, where the tone is set by both players and audience, and where music, drink, and talk combine to create a special mood. As one publican put it: "The drink attracts the musicians and the musicians attract the drinkers."

A "session" in a pub can be sparked spontaneously by musicians who frequent certain pubs, knowing they'll find each other, or it can be a scheduled event. Either way, the music-making usually proceeds quite informally, with none of the packaged flavor of prearranged sets. The instruments are tin whistle, Uilleann pipes, concertina, fiddle, bodhran (a cross between a drum and a tambourine), and harp.

There is a subtle etiquette to a session: one player will start a tune that he or she thinks the others can join in on. If no one does join in, the player will stop, not wanting to be rude. It's then good form for the others to insist, and to tease the player into continuing the solo, and equally good form for the player to shyly demur before finally giving in.

Often a session will include a *sean nos* singer, a soloist who performs without accompaniment, the style very quiet, very expressive, with a twisting melodic line.

As the momentum picks up with the increasing flow of "spirits" both alcoholic and jovial, the music gets better and better, till by closing time it is bringing down the house, with the musicians bathed in sweat and the crowd singing and clapping. The barman has a hard time getting people out and has to become severe, turning out lights and intoning sternly, "Time, ladies and gentlemen, time."

Since the musicians and the audience are all warmed up, it's not unusual for everyone to spill over to restaurants and cafés to continue the fun in places that are licensed to close later, or in the back rooms of pubs that stay open illegally. If the mix is right, people will even repair to someone's house for a singsong.

Though there is music to be heard in every corner of Ireland, the best concentration of pubs with really good musicians is naturally in Dublin. Here you can hear a truly amazing array of styles from disco to rock to Uilleann pipes.

A few years ago, several young Irish musicians who grew up influenced by blues and rock as well as traditional Irish music began to fuse the new with the old. The result was an exciting mix that became an international hit, a kind of "trad-rock." Horslips was the most popular of these groups, and Planxty and Paul Brady are also well known.

The most famous Irish band is The Chieftains, a traditional group of tremendous verve and energy. They are a delightfully motley crew, both in age and demeanor, who started by playing together in their spare time. When they went professional, Paddy Maloney commented: "After all, we look terrible on stage in our sweaters and suits. We don't jump around, we have no gimmicks, and we don't even have any metallic instruments except the steel strings on the harp. But it seems that people are listening to music more now. And we don't want to just play to folk audiences. We wanted to play to rock audiences—the lot."

The Chieftains' universal appeal lies in the sheer quality of their playing, and in the fact that their music allows for improvisation. It varies from ancient melodies, including compositions by O'Carolan, played on the pipes, the fiddle, or the harp, to passages as delicately arranged as chamber music, to boisterous jigs and reels. It's tranquil but exciting, modern but timeless.

But it isn't only listening to famous bands or sitting in on sessions that will acquaint you with Ireland's music. Everyone in Ireland sings. For a while in the 1940s and '50s, pubs sprouted NO SINGING signs, but as with many official things in Ireland, this edict disappeared. Popular "trad-rock" performer Paul Brady comments:

I'm a musician who was trained as a classical pianist. I've played rock and roll, I've played electric guitars, I've played traditional music straight with traditional musicians in sessions on tin whistle. I don't want to be labelled as one sort of musician or another. I believe that the vast majority of people of my age in this country have as much American culture in them as Irish culture and I don't see why this is necessarily some kind of original sin that must be cleansed before one can truly be an Irish person. I don't see why, if you're creating music, you should necessarily have to restrict yourself and refuse to let these things mingle. I just want to take what I love and feel from traditional music into my consciousness.

A SELECTION OF IRELAND'S
MOST POPULAR MUSICIANS ON RECORD AND TAPE

The Chieftains	Tommy Makem
Horslips	Planxty
The Dubliners	Christy Moore
Van Morrison	Davy Arthur
Andy Irvine and Paul Brady	The Bothy Band
Rory Gallagher	Tom Paxton
The Fury Brothers	Oisin
The Clancy Brothers	Davey Hammond

LEINSTER

County Dublin

County Wicklow

County Wexford

County Westmeath

County Kildare

County Kilkenny

County Offaly

County Longford

County Meath

County Louth

County Laois

County Carlow

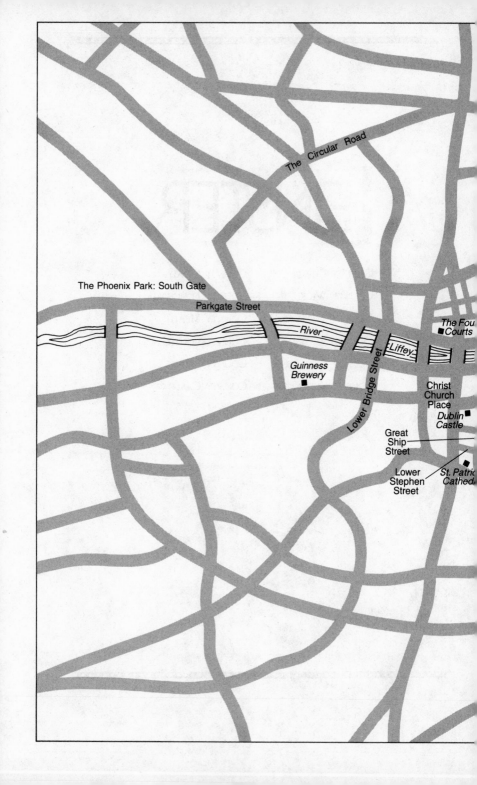

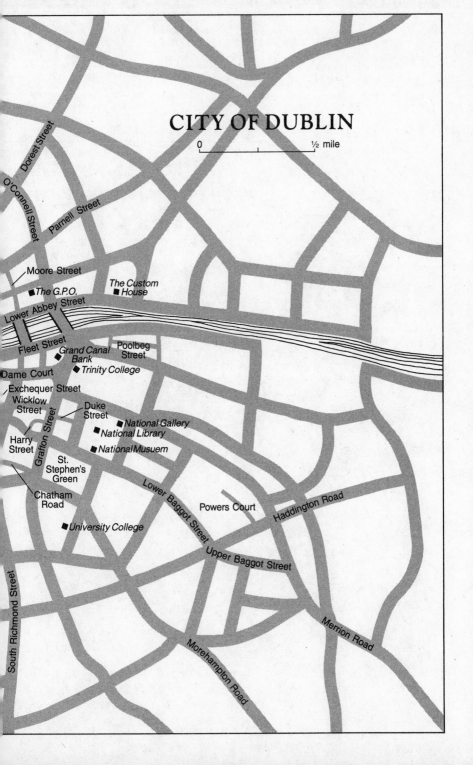

CITY OF DUBLIN

0 ½ mile

Dorest Street

O'Connell Street

Parnell Street

Moore Street

■ The G.P.O.

The Custom
■ House

Lower Abbey Street

Fleet Street

Grand Canal
■ Bank

Poolbeg
Street

Dame Court

◆ Trinity College

Exchequer Street

Wicklow
Street

Duke
Street

■ National Gallery

■ National Library

Harry
Street

Grafton Street

■ National Musuem

St.
Stephen's
Green

Chatham
Road

Lower Baggot Street

Powers Court

Haddington Road

■ University College

Upper Baggot Street

South Richmond Street

Merrion Road

Morehampton Road

Dublin, Wicklow, Louth, and a small portion of Meath are coastal counties, but the rest of Leinster is inland, forming what is known as the midlands.

Ireland is basically an undulating central plain of limestone encircled by a coastal belt of highlands. The central plain is covered with peat bog and glacial deposits of sand and clay, and dotted with numerous lakes. The river Shannon drains this area into a basin which, surprisingly enough, covers one-fifth of the country.

COUNTY DUBLIN

DUBLIN

Dublin is the great mother of all Irish pubs. When you first come to Dublin you can almost believe that the town was invented as an excuse for the creation of pubs. There is a pub for every occasion, from funeral to dart contest, and for every kind of person, from barrister to fisherman. There are even pubs that mix all these elements together. A word of warning: It is possible to so enjoy pub crawling in Dublin that you endlessly postpone departure.

Though we know the lovely, crescent-shaped harbor of Dublin existed in A.D. 140—the Macedonian historian Ptolemy referred to it as Eblana—it was born as a bona fide town in A.D. 841, when the Vikings invaded Ireland and brought with them the concepts of towns and commerce.

The Norsemen called their new port Dubh Linn, the Black Pool, and parts of the walled city they established still remain for the romantic traveler to examine. If you want animated proof of the Vikings' Irish adventure, walk down Grafton Street, Dublin's main drag, or enter a variety of pubs: you will encounter quite a few blue eyes and red beards.

The next major attempt to subdue Ireland was at the hands of the Anglo-Normans; Dublin was a Norman stronghold during the Middle Ages. Surviving the fires, plagues, and rebellions that ravaged her during that period, she became "Dublin's Fair City" under English dominion with the firm establishment of the Ascendancy. The governing English and Anglo-Irish built the tranquil parks and classic Georgian façades that so characterize the city.

But as with many façades, the gracious veneer covered an ugly reality in the teeming horror of Dublin's slums, areas like the Liberties, so named with unintentional irony. The slavery and poverty produced men passionately devoted to the idea of Irish freedom; one might even say they were the first urban guerrillas.

In 1798, inspired by the French Revolution, Wolfe Tone led the first abortive revolt against British rule. From then on, such acts of rebellion were repeated continuously, bubbling up from an enslaved, deprived, starving populace on the one hand and the outrage of the revolutionary members of the Ascendancy on the other (see page 219). Finally, on Easter Monday, 1916, at Dublin's General Post Office on O'Connell Street, a small band of men rose up: their subsequent martyrdom led to the creation of the Irish Free State in 1922.

This, of course, is a presentation so encapsulated and devoid of the complexities and paradoxes common to anything Irish that it would guarantee an immediate discussion in just about any pub. However, it gives you a starting point.

As you wander through Dublin, you'll find Ireland's history present in the names of the streets and the numerous statues. Justly known as the largest village in the world, Dublin's structure is organic rather than mechanical. Her people, buildings, streets, and pubs are living history, like the rings of a tree. In a sense, Dublin's appeal resides in the fact that it is still a town on the human scale. With a 1982 population of 384,806, people can and do know one another well; they greet one another in the streets and pubs. Human beings are not dwarfed by their own creations.

In the deep tranquillity of St. Stephen's Green, the park made famous by James Joyce, time slows as you watch the swans in the lake and the strolling students from nearby Trinity College. It is easy to enter the rhythm of a bygone era, to feel the ghosts of the great Irish writers whose ambience now surrounds you: Shaw and Yeats, Joyce and Wilde, Sheridan and O'Casey, Behan and Beckett.

Here in Ireland's capital, where so much legend is concentrated, where the famous and often lethal Irish combination of drink and talk has flowered into great literature and enduring wit, it is easy to wax romantic. But the Dubliner, a born romantic himself, will not let you get carried away. "In Ireland," said Sean O'Faolain, "it is bad taste to be serious." And the Dubliner would agree.

ABBEY MOONEY
1 Lower Abbey Street
Food: Full menu   *Specialty:* Curry

Walking along Lower Abbey Street, a scone's throw from the river Liffey, you'll be hard-pressed not to enter the Abbey Mooney once you've looked in. The ground floor is vast and uncluttered, and the shining mahogany and stained glass is *de rigueur* Dublin pub splendor; but the wonderful birthday-cake folly of the ceiling is something you'll not find again soon. The elaborate curlicues of painted plaster garlands have looked down on generations, including some of Ireland's finest writers, who have immortalized the place in their works.

Here Beckett's Neary "sat all day until he had completed the circuit of the counters, when he would start all over again in the reverse direction." Here, too, Joyce's Stephen Dedalus came to take in a noontime jar with his cronies from the press.

The upstairs lounges, "O'Casey" and "Yeats," in honor of the two major playwrights of the Abbey Theatre, which is close by, are equally grandiose.

THE BAGGOT MOONEY
2 Upper Baggot Street

One of the Mooney clan of pubs, this imposing Victorian building dominates a corner of the Baggot Street Bridge, which spans the Grand Canal.

In the nineteenth century, light barges towed by horses ferried passengers over the Irish canal and waterway system between Dublin and the river Shannon. These "flyboats," as they were called, were often delightfully decorated with gold leaf and bright paint, and to travel along these "liquid roads" must have been a slow but sure pleasure.

Though the barges are gone, the canal still has its uses. In a sense, when you swallow a delicious draught of Guinness you are taking the very water of Dublin, since Guinness is brewed with the water of the Grand Canal, Lock 8 to be exact. According to the experts, it is the quality of the water used which makes the brew special; in this case, water from the northern and western slopes of the Dublin Mountains.

For a nostalgic walk, take the towpath along the canal, with its grassy banks, old bridges, and shady trees. At the Baggot Street Bridge, "sit for a spell" on the stone bench which commemorates the satiric Irish poet and writer Patrick Kavanagh. The bench is near the canal locks where Kavanagh often sat; it was erected by his friends in accordance with the request he made in his poem "Lines Written on a Seat on the Grand Canal, Dublin":

> O commemorate me where there is water,
> Canal water preferably, so stilly
> Greenly at the heart of summer.
> O commemorate me with no hero-courageous
> Tomb—just a canal-bank seat for the passer-by.

This area of the city has many offices, and across the bridge from Mooney's is the glass-and-steel home of the Irish Tourist Board, or Bord Failte (Board of the Welcomes). Pick up some copies of their very beautiful magazine, *Ireland of the Welcomes*, and peruse them at Mooney's.

Mooney's is old-fashioned, high-ceilinged, and cavernous. From the windows of the upstairs bar the view overlooks the canal; downstairs are two bars, one rather dark and TV-oriented, the other lit by large, multipaned windows.

I had a twilight drink there with an editor who was in complete sympathy with my infatuation with the light and landscape of Ireland; but when I spoke of moving there, she smiled wryly and warned against that common tourist pitfall, romanticizing. I told her that I was well aware of the drawbacks, such as dreary, wet winters and the abysmal Irish telephone system, but that to me Ireland's magic was stronger than her discomforts.

Perhaps this lady had seen one too many sweet dreams of thatched cottages go sour: yet it was she who said, "I have an intense physical relationship to the land . . . I wouldn't *be* if I were anywhere else on earth."

THE BAILEY
2–3 Duke Street

A short history of the Bailey provides the best possible starting point from which to view Irish life and Irish personalities—literary, social, and political.

The Bailey began modestly enough as an eating house in 1837. Gradually it became a meeting place for the brightest minds and wits of Ireland until, at the turn of the century, it had turned into a kind of super-pub, the ideal of Irish pubdom. The pronouncements and quips delivered over a pint at The Bailey would soon be repeated all over Dublin. "They would sacrifice their own mother for a witty phrase," is how one contemporary described it.

Ulick O'Connor, the well-known writer, has compared The Bailey in its heyday to The Mermaid Tavern of Elizabethan England:

The Bailey has points of comparison with The Mermaid Tavern, the reputation of a heady phrase on the general mouth, the recitation of a verse casually composed about some current event. . . . In those years, the pace of life in Dublin left plenty of room for tongue-wagging. Any event of note in the city was sure to unleash its chain of anecdotes and be embroidered by the wits and raconteurs as soon as it reached their eager ears.

At The Bailey, the passion that Dubliners have for clinical observation and exploration of character was given full reign. Local personalities were incorporated into anecdotes, illustrative of their personal idiosyncrasies or eccentricities. It did not matter if the tales concerned friends of the group discussing them. The artist's license was allowed to the teller of the tale.

The hub around which the Bailey group revolved was Arthur Griffith. He was the founder of Sinn Fein (Ourselves Alone), which from 1906 advocated a separate parliament and a massive program of industrialization. Along with two or three others, Arthur Griffith created the basis for the modern Irish state. Most of the writers of the Irish literary renaissance—W. B. Yeats, Padraic Colum, James Stephens, et al.— wrote for Griffith's newspaper, *The United Irishman.*

Though Churchill noted that Griffith was "that unusual figure, a silent Irishman," Griffith was a good listener and created an ambience in which wit and conversation thrived. He was also an accomplished balladeer and on special occasions would sing his "Ballad of the Thirteenth Lock," a song about a haunted bargeman which is frequently sung today, but which few know was composed by Griffith.

The upstairs room where Griffith held sway has a history as an unofficial center for political as well as literary ferment. Tradition has it that Parnell and members of the Irish Party came here, and that it was also used as a meeting place by the secret revolutionary group, the Invincibles.

Michael Collins, the legendary IRA general, came to The Bailey when he was on the run from the Black and Tans, a special force of British ex-servicemen so called because of their mixed police-and-military uniform. Collins visited The Bailey only at lunchtime and went straight upstairs, because of the presence of the British military in the bar in the evenings.

Since it attracted a literary set, there are many references to The Bailey in works by well-known writers. James Stephens, author of *The Crock of Gold,* a tale of philosophy and leprechauns, remembers his first visit there:

Upon an evening I found myself sitting in the Bailey in front of a drink. I had my first adventure in the air, oxygen and gin, which we call wit, and which I watched as a cat watches a mouse, meaning to catch it, and for the first time I heard poetry spoken of with the assured carelessness with which a carpenter talks of his planks and of the chairs and tables and oddments he will make them with.

Oliver St. John Gogarty, the writer, surgeon, airman, and famed conversationalist, remembered The Bailey as "The Museum of Dublin because it is the House of the Muses."

It was also the house of the individual. Colorful characters abounded, my favorite being Valentine Nolan-Whelan. Valentine was a barrister and bon vivant. Twice he broke the bank at Monte Carlo. He liked to buy unusual underwear for his girlfriends; but this could not have been the reason he was constantly broke, as he had, aside from his earnings at the casino and race courses, a considerable private income. When he did finally go broke, he did it with style: while entertaining at dinner he enjoined the butler at each course to "make sure the boys are well fed." Who were the boys? The bailiffs who were at that moment removing the furniture from some of the other rooms.

With the death of the owner, William Hogan, in 1945, The Bailey became more of a fashionable eating house, catering to international names such as Margot Fonteyn, Charlie Chaplin, Peter Ustinov, and Evelyn Waugh.

I will now practice the colorful gambit of the "aside," a technique you will frequently encounter in the labyrinthean conventions of Irish conversation. Speaking of Evelyn Waugh, Brendan Behan tells a great pub story in *Brendan Behan's Island: An Irish Sketchbook:* "There's a pub up near Guinness's Brewery on the Liffey Quay—it must be the nearest pub to Guinness's—known as 'The Shaky Man.' I don't know if it's there now or not because it's been a long time since I was in it, but I think it was there I heard one of my friends—a man named Crippen—refer to 'Evelyn Warr.' 'Aye,' he said, 'Evelyn Warr was a tough woman . . . and,' says he, 'she was a great soldier and a great warrior. And she was called Evelyn because that was her name and she was called Warr because she was all for war.' "

And speaking of Brendan Behan (now I'm going to get back to the original subject without skipping a beat, a skill also acquired in Dublin pubs), he too was a frequent imbiber at The Bailey, part of the literary crowd that was to reappear under the ownership of John Ryan, 1958–

71. John Ryan, himself an artist and a man of letters, created the ambience that drew the likes of Myles na Gopaleen, J. P. Donleavy (*The Ginger Man*), and Patrick Kavanagh.

But The Bailey's most famous literary patron was probably James Joyce, and the pub is now the repository for a fine piece of Joyceiana. As you mount the stairs inside the pub, you are faced with a blue door marked with the number 7 and flanked by two gas lamps. This is the actual door to 7 Eccles Street, immortalized by Joyce as the house of Leopold Bloom in *Ulysses*. The house was, in fact, the home of his friend John Francis Byrne, who was to become Crawley in *Portrait of the Artist as a Young Man*. (It was demolished in 1967.) In addition to the door, you may also inspect such memorabilia as Michael Collins's revolver, Brendan Behan's tankard, an original portrait from life of Robert Emmet, Lord Edward Fitzgerald's portrait and signature, and an entire display devoted to Patrick Kavanagh.

BOWES
2 Fleet Street
This is the hangout for the newspaper crowd since Bowes is especially handy to those who labor for *The Irish Times*, whose offices are just a few doors away. This warmly lit pub, with its dark, coffered walls and photographs of Dublin, is a good place for creative eavesdropping. In the front are two snugs with milk-glass walls from which come periodic bursts of laughter.

Since Ireland is supposed to represent the apogee of the written and spoken word, it is not surprising that a stupendous amount of verbiage pours off the printing presses and into books, magazines, and newspapers, and that newspapers are a very important part of Irish life.

In a country of 5 million people, there are no less than seven daily morning papers—at least three of which could be called national dailies—three daily evening papers, and four Sunday papers. Each province (Ulster, Leinster, Munster, and Connacht) has its own paper, published at least once a week, and there is a long list of weekly provincial newspapers, too. All seem to command a good readership, and nearly all these newspapers are well produced and well written.

THE BRAZEN HEAD
20 Lower Bridge Street

This is Dublin's oldest drinking establishment. The Brazen Head was formally chartered in 1688, but a place for refreshing the weary traveler has existed on this spot probably since the twelfth century.

You can find The Brazen Head on the west side of Bridge Street, but be on the alert for it, as it is easily overlooked. Watch for a low archway. This will lead you through a tunnel and then to a small courtyard of broken flagstones that have resounded to the arrivals and departures of Viking horsemen, Strongbow's Norman adventurers, Swift's fellow students, and Robert Emmet's gentlemen revolutionaries.

Inside, the uneven planes of floors and walls attest further to the pub's antiquity. Keep to the right after you enter; a long dark corridor will lead you to a close, low-ceilinged room filled with shadowy corners where patrons talk quietly.

Little has changed here since 1790, when it was a rendezvous for Wolfe Tone, Lord Edward Fitzgerald, and the United Irishmen. Robert Emmet, the revered patriot who was hanged for leading the insurrection of 1803, lodged in a room above, and his writing desk is kept by the bar.

BRIAN BORU HOUSE
Finglas Road
Glasnevin

Funerals are important social occasions in Ireland; while the old-fashioned twenty-four-hour wake, complete with hired mourners called keeners, is now found only in the remoter regions, funeral parties still gather after a burial for a heavy session of food and drink.

The Brian Boru on the Finglas Road to Glasnevin Cemetery is a popular stop for Dublin funeral corteges, serving as a kind of decompression chamber between the grief of the burial and the return home to Dublin.

James Joyce records the route of such a procession in *Ulysses*, and Brendan Behan records a marvelous cameo of two drunks in the cemetery:

They asked for Mulcahy of the Coombe and were told where he was buried. After traipsing about in the fog, they found the grave, sure enough. One of the drunks spelt out the name: Terrence Mulcahy. The other drunk was blinking up at a statue of Our Saviour the widow had got put up . . . and, after blinking up at the sacred figure, "Not a bloody bit like the man," says he: "That's not Mulcahy," says he, "whoever done it."

DAVY BYRNES
21 Duke Street
Food: Good pub grub as well as hot pies

"He entered Davy Byrnes. Moral pub." So James Joyce refers to Davy Byrnes in *Ulysses.* Entering it yourself, you may still get a feel for what was meant by that slightly enigmatic description. Although the pub has undergone major changes since Joyce immortalized it, it remains a friendly and excellent place to catch the modern versions of Joyce's "Dubliners." Situated on Duke Street off Dawson, the pub is in the exact center of the city, a convenient meeting place.

There are three bars: the main bar, the Ulysses Bar, and the main lounge, which used to be the famous "back room." The Ulysses Bar has a handy entrance from Grafton Street (the shopping center) through the Creation Arcade, a jumble of shops.

Though the place has been unaggressively modernized, some links with the old days remain. In the Ulysses Bar is a remarkable engraved mirror showing the upper yard of Dublin Castle in 1880. With bottles and glasses standing before it, the effect is interestingly surreal, especially if you are under the influence of the "Davy Byrnes special."

In the main bar are some captivating murals. One, of a 1920s bucolic bacchanal in the idyllic Irish countryside, includes a portrait of Davy Byrnes, nattily attired, sitting under a tree. His expression, that of a slightly bemused, interested bystander thoughtfully overseeing the whole scene, must certainly have been drawn from life. Somehow this mural recalls an apocryphal story in which a young man, having already visited several of the local watering holes, finds himself in one with a barmaid. When she asks him his preference, he waxes courtly, saying, "A jug of wine, a loaf of bread, and thou," to which she replies "Who do you think Kiam?"

Davy Byrnes himself must have become inured to many such stories over the fifty years he presided behind the bar. As a young Wicklow-man, he came to Dublin in 1873 to seek his fortune; and since the repu-tation of a pub is made not so much on the strength of its physical properties as on the character of its owner, a list of Davy Byrnes's clien-tele becomes an interesting tribute to "yer man" himself.

THE CHINAMAN
28 Great Ship Street
Now, I'm not saying that it does, but this pub has been reputed to stay open till 2:00 a.m. The reason for this is that it is the hangout of the police. It is situated across from the notorious Kilmainham Jail (where so many patriots were incarcerated) and behind Dublin Castle. One might say it is between the rock and the hard place.

The Chinaman is a rough-and-ready old place with plenty of action. I met an actor and writer here named Alan, who said to me with typical Irish mockery, "The Celts invented two things, whiskey and self-destruction." *Slainte!*

CONWAY'S
70 Parnell Street
Food: Pub grub
A winner in the National Bar Food competition, Conway's offers a great variety of excellent pub grub. The most striking thing about the decor is an intricate central structure encircled by the bar, which was built to contain all the bottles, glasses, and gewgaws. This structure is made of carved wood and resembles a maverick, miniature Gothic ca-thedral.

Conway's is the haunt of obstetricians from the Rotunda Maternity Hospital opposite. They have their own call system, and it's hard to know whether they are celebrating a successful birth or whiling away the time before a delivery.

DOHENY & NESBITT
5 Lower Baggot Street
This pub is probably one of the most popular in Dublin for all genera-tions. After you've seen its perfect antique frontage and the polished brass sign advertising TEA AND WINE MERCHANT, it will come as no sur-

prise to you that the pub is 130 years old and carrying its age beautifully, thank you.

I'm pleased to report that the interior completely lives up to the exterior, a happy harmony that isn't all that common in life. Pass through
the swinging doors and you'll find yourself in authentic early-Victorian
surroundings complete with high ceilings, old whiskey casks, pumps
and tankards, wooden partitions, marble-topped tables, and antique
mirrors. The wooden partitions serve to create intimate islands in the
impressive sea of people of all sorts.

The place is so "packed out" that the management has been forced to
open up more space upstairs. Study the barmen for a fine example of
the art of Dublin bartending.

I was first introduced to Doheny & Nesbitt during the day, when,
like most Dublin pubs and people, it offers an entirely different face.
The feeling is lazy and easy, the barman is tending to maintenance,
polishing this and that, and there is time and peace for artful conversation.

I went there one morning at 11:30 with one of the finest nonstop
raconteurs in Ireland, the admirable writer and chronicler, Benedict
Kiely. He can blend one story into another as effortlessly as one pint
flows into the next as you listen.

After a while an American journalist wandered in. He had come to
Dublin on a vacation fifteen years earlier and was still there. Immediately the two men became enmeshed in a discussion of minute Irish historical detail that left me miles behind. The journalist departed, and
with just a pause for a sip, Ben flowed easily into the next story.

I do remember the pint-drinkers' club in a certain back room. For initiation you had to drink seventeen pints, one after the other, and then buy a
round for everyone in sight. The rules were framed on the wall. Membership was naturally exclusive.

Opening off the back room was a sort of hallway with a blind stairway,
roofed over to make a larger room above. The great joke was to send a
half-tipsy stranger in there looking for the Gents and then listen atten-
tively for the thump as he ascended the truncated stairway on the road to
nowhere and his head made contact with the ceiling and he came reeling
out again. I was a victim once. The echoes of the laughter are with me
still.

BARTLEY DUNNE'S
32 Lower Stephen Street
Food: Pub grub—range of cold plates
Bartley Dunne's definitely has "atmosphere." It is candlelit and has soft piped-in music. The predominant feeling is Modern Victoriana. To the right is a long bar and to the left a series of niches creating an intimate environment for leisurely drinking.

Mr. Dunne, the proprietor, will provide you with any drink you want or can imagine, provided you know its ingredients.

IRISH SODA BREAD

Traditional. Irish soda bread is one of the specialties of the country and is still baked in countless farmhouses and homes all over Ireland. It is made in white or brown loaves, the latter being made from whole-wheat flour. It is very easy to make.

White
1½ lb. (6 cups) flour
½ pt. (1 cup, approx.) buttermilk, sour milk, or fresh milk; if the last,
 1 tea. cream of tartar is added to dry ingredients
1 tea. baking soda
1 tea. salt

Mix the dry ingredients together in a large bowl and make a well in the center. Add enough milk to make a thick dough. Stir with a wooden spoon; the pouring should be done in large quantities, not spoonful by spoonful. The mixture should be slack but not wet and the mixing done lightly and quickly. Add a little more milk if it seems too stiff. With floured hands put onto a lightly floured board or table and flatten the dough into a circle about 1½ inches thick. Put on a baking sheet, and make a large cross on the top with a floured knife. (This is to ensure even distribution of heat.) Bake in a moderate to hot oven (375°F.–400°F.) about forty minutes. Test the center with a skewer before removing from the oven. To keep the bread soft, wrap it in a clean tea towel. This quantity will make 1 large loaf or 2 small ones.

In the back room, which has niches as well as tables, you can enjoy a good selection of cold-meat platters as well as wine from the most extensive list in Dublin. The host ships his own wine in case you want to leave with a bottle.

The gathering there is varied and predominantly gay. The casual visitor is rather overtly studied, but if you can withstand all those eyes it's worth a try to experience the unusual in Dublin night life.

THE HENRY GRATTAN
44 Lower Baggot Street
Specialty: Homemade chicken liver
This is a new pub devoted to political satire. It is furnished in the old style, with the additional comforts of carpeting and cushioning.

Michael Tierney, a banker with the Allied Irish Bank, is the owner-manager responsible for the skillful decorating job. He has used old materials from everywhere: timbers from an ocean liner, bar front from a 147-year-old Provincial Bank, wainscotting from old tellers' cubbies, old bar mirrors, and the mahogany counter from the famous, now sadly defunct Princess Bar. (Get the barman to tell you about it.)

Downstairs is a fine brass bar and a dining room called "Man Bites Dog," named in honor of the acerbic column that appears Tuesdays in *The Irish Times*, written by political satirist Donal Foley. The food is excellent and the clientele mainly businessmen and pretty secretaries.

Wander around and look at the cartoons on the wall. They'll give you a biting insight into Irish political history.

Henry Grattan, after whom the pub is named, was an eloquent eighteenth-century leader of the Irish Parliament. In 1782, he fought for and won independence from the English Parliament, a first step in the struggle for freedom from British domination.

THE HOLE IN THE WALL
The Phoenix Park
South Gate
The Hole in the Wall is a bit more elegant than the picture conjured up

by its name. It's a long series of connecting rooms, comfortably appointed in traditional-modern but not objectionable style, a pleasant place. The best thing about it is its location smack against the wall of the Phoenix Park. (For some reason, Dubliners never refer simply to Phoenix Park, it's always *the* Phoenix Park.)

The Phoenix Park is one of Dublin's great treasures and not to be missed. Less than two miles from the center of the city, it is very popular both winter and summer. Several dignitaries are fortunate enough to make their headquarters here: the President of Ireland, the Papal Nuncio, and the American ambassador have as a common front yard the park's 1,760 acres of pure verdant delight.

Its meadows and forests have also served Dubliners as garden and playground since 1747, when the Royal Deer Park was thrown open to the public by the Earl of Chesterfield, viceroy at the time. Through the lush green center of the park runs a magnificent three-mile drive bordered by fine chestnut trees, majestic oaks, and groves of hawthorn and silvery birches. If you're lucky, you'll catch a glimpse of the herd of deer that browse in the fields beside the road.

Next to the drive is a column bearing a sculpted phoenix, the miraculous bird that rises reborn from its own ashes. The Phoenix Park was named after this bird through a kind of slip of the tongue: "phoenix" is what emerged from the Gaelic "*fionn uisage,*" which actually means "clear water." The water referred to is a mineral spring near the north end of the Zoological Gardens.

The Zoological Gardens are "grand" from the first moment you enter, which you do through a whimsical thatched gatehouse, the epitome of all gatehouses, built, or rather invented, in 1833. The zoo opened in 1831, which makes it the third oldest in the world after London and Paris. There have been considerable changes since, when the only resident was a wild boar. Now all the usual denizens of zoos are there, living in exquisitely landscaped gardens surrounding a mirror-smooth pond. Just to add a finishing touch, colorful flamingos, peacocks, cranes, and pelicans wander around like living jewels in the leafy green.

Brendan Behan was particularly fond of the park and especially of the zoo. He even composed a poem in honor of it.

I brought me mot up to the zoo
For to show her the lion and the kangaroo;
There were he-males and she-males of each shade and hue
Inside the Zoological Gardens.
I went up there on my honeymoon;
We saw the giraffe and the hairy baboon,
There were parrots and larks and two doves all a-cooing
Inside the Zoological Gardens.

   Trouble and strife, it is no lark,
   Dublin city is in the dark;
   You want to get out to the Phoenix Park
   And view the Zoological Gardens.

"Oh," says she, "me darling Jack
I'd love a ride on the elephant's back,"
"If you don't ge' ou' a that, I'll give you such a crack
Up in the Zoological Gardens."
As I went up by the old Parkgate
The polisman was upon his bate
And tried to make love to me darling Kate
Inside the Zoological Gardens.

   Trouble and strife, it is no lark,
   Dublin city is in the dark;
   You want to get out to the Phoenix Park
   And view the Zoological Gardens.

"Don't drag me like that or you'll ruin me frock."
"If you don't hurry up, Dunphy's door will be locked,
I can hear the bells ringing for seven o'clock
Inside the Zoological Gardens."
At Dunphy's corner the tram did stop.
We were just in time to get in for a drop
And I kissed her one of the real old stock
Outside the Zoological Gardens.

   Trouble and strife, it is no lark,
   Dublin city is in the dark;
   You want to get out to the Phoenix Park
   And view the Zoological Gardens.

THE INTERNATIONAL BAR
23 Wicklow Street
Food: Pub grub

Like many Dublin pubs, this one is situated on a corner, probably so you can be trapped both coming and going. It is a time capsule of the nineteenth century, which is not surprising since it has been owned and operated by the same family, the Donohoes, since 1888.

The high ceilings, the massive marble-topped bar and mahogany bar furniture, the brass rails, plants, and endless mirrors give you a sense of opulent ease, and the mysterious caryatides along the mirror are fun and a nice reminder of Old World classicism. The host is very friendly and doesn't mind sharing his stories and information. The pint pulled here is reputed to be excellent. The "crowd" is youngish and fashionable.

There is a pleasant cellar downstairs.

KAVANAGH'S
1 Prospect Square
Glasnevin

Next to the back gate of Glasnevin Cemetery is Kavanagh's, in business since 1833. The proprietor, John, is the eighth generation of Kavanaghs to slake the thirst not only of the regulars but also of tired grave-diggers seeking a refreshing pint.

This pub is one of the best-preserved examples of the "traditional" Irish pub, untouched by that faint whiff of the museum that a restored pub sometimes gives off. Though it has been used as a favorite location for pub shots in many films, it is a real-honest-to-God-genuine working pub, as attested to by the sawdust, the unyielding light, and the swinging doors isolating you cozily in your worn wooden snug. The long main room doesn't seem as large as it actually is, since it's divided and partitioned into a variety of cubbyholes and lurking places for comradely drinking and talk.

Around ten in the evening, the place is buzzing, but it's not as crowded as the pubs in the center city, or "Joycecity." The crowd is composed of all ages and occupations. If you can get John Kavanagh's attention for a few minutes, you'll find that in addition to pulling one of the better pints in Dublin, he's an excellent storyteller and a fast man with the words. It's possible to find yourself just catching the joke and beginning to laugh when he's already moved into the next bit of banter. This is something you'll encounter often in Irish conversation.

Kavanagh's connection with Glasnevin Cemetery is more than just proximity—the pub actually has a small opening in one of the walls adjoining the cemetery grounds through which it was customary for thirsty gravediggers to pass a shovel. A pint was placed on the shovel, and the work went on much enlivened.

Most people call Dublin's main cemetery Glasnevin after the suburb it's located in, and they probably wouldn't know what you were talking about if you referred to it by its real name, Prospect Cemetery. By either name, it is the quintessential graveyard, ideal for a ruminative, elegiac wander among its dark cypress trees and melancholy yews, its angels, pillars, crosses, and vaults. (And if you want to ramble farther, among flowers and trees, next door are the Botanic Gardens.)

Many of Ireland's illustrious names lie buried here. As you enter the main gate you'll see a full-size replica of an ancient Irish round tower. During the Norse invasions of A.D. 852–1000 these were built as lookout points and refuges for the Cistercian monks whose monastic enclaves were beacons of learning for the Europe of the Dark Ages.

This particular tower is a monument to Daniel O'Connell, the dynamic statesman and persuasive orator, the first Irishman to sit in an English Parliament.

A short distance away is a large granite boulder with a giant PARNELL chiseled on it, for though Charles Stewart Parnell was a Protestant, he was granted burial in this Catholic cemetery.

Other Irish patriots who rest here are Michael Collins, the handsome young general and driving force of the "Rising," tragically killed in an ambush during the Civil War of 1922; Eamon De Valera, the New York–born President of Ireland from 1959 to 1973; and Jeremiah O'Donovan Rossa, whose revolutionary activities against the British earned him years in jail and this famous graveside eulogy by Padraic Pearse, with the ringing and oft-quoted exhortation to resist British domination: "They have left us our Fenian dead, and while Ireland holds these graves, Ireland unfree shall never be at peace."

Maybe you'll hear a mocking laugh, the ghostly mirth of Brendan

Behan, who is buried here; and oh, yes, not to be forgotten is Barry Fitzgerald, who began his career at the famous Abbey Theatre, and whose stage-Irish character acting was to represent the Irish to millions of moviegoers the world over. With all due respect to Barry, people in Ireland don't really say, "Top o' the mornin' to ya."

THE LORD EDWARD TAVERN
23 Christ Church Place
Lunch: 12:30–2:30   *Dinner:* 6:00–10:45. Restaurant closed Sunday
Specialty: Seafood

Built by the present owner's grandfather a hundred years ago, it stands on the site of previous taverns dating back to the Middle Ages. It is in the oldest part of the "walled city," a short step from several historic spots. This famous tavern is named after Lord Edward Fitzgerald. Lord Edward reached high rank in the English Army, and saw service in the American and West Indian colonies. He was a son of the Duke of Leinster (his town house was Leinster House, now the seat of the Dail), and he was regularly received at the Court of St. James's in London. On his return to Ireland, he was given a seat in the Irish Parliament, but it did not take him long to realize that this was a puppet parliament. Disillusioned with their policy rigging, he soon came to the notice of the United Irishmen (Free Ireland Movement). Because of his military experience he was appointed commander-in-chief of their forces, and helped plan the abortive rebellion of 1798 against the crown with Robert Emmet, Wolfe Tone, and Napper-Tandy. Due to the ever-present paid informer of the crown in Ireland's long history of insurrection, Lord Edward was arrested in his hiding place in nearby Thomas Street, prior to the date fixed for the rebellion. In resisting arrest, he was severely wounded and later died of his wounds in Newgate prison at the age of thirty-five.

Tom Cunniam, who manages The Lord Edward, has Irish insurgent history running through his veins: the Cunniam family had strong connections with the United Irishmen in Wicklow, where one of them was executed for his part in the 1798 Rebellion. They were also involved with the Fenian Movement of 1867.

The Lord Edward can be enjoyed literally on several levels: on the ground floor is a fine Dublin pub of character, rather small, dark, and intimate; the first-floor bar specializes in excellent pub grub and boasts an open fire in winter; the second floor is the place for fine meals of fresh fish, smoked salmon, and Dublin Bay prawns.

CHRIST CHURCH CATHEDRAL

The cathedral, which was founded over a thousand years ago by the Danish ruler of Dublin, Sitric III, serves the Protestant archdiocese of Dublin and Glendalough. It is the oldest building in Dublin and the final resting place of the famous Norman crusader Strongbow, who rebuilt it in 1172. His grave is marked with a stone effigy of a recumbent knight in black chain mail. Beside the fierce Norman leader lies the diminutive statue of his son, cut off at the waist. A sad legend has it that Strongbow was so enraged at the cowardice of his son in battle against the hostile Irish tribesmen that he struck him in half with his powerful sword.

There is a ghostly crypt consisting of arches and huge foundation stones stretching the entire length of the church. In this, the oldest part of the building, you can see the candlesticks and tabernacle used in 1689, when Mass was celebrated with James II in attendance. The church seems to have attracted kings: in 1487 Lambert Simnel, the Yorkish pretender to the throne of England, was crowned King Edward VI, as a rival to Henry VII.

Should you be in Dublin on New Year's Eve, go to the cathedral at midnight. As the bells peal out, celebrants dance in giddy circles around the church as far out as O'Connell Bridge.

ST. PATRICK'S CATHEDRAL

This corner of Dublin is rife with the memory of Jonathan Swift, dean of St. Patrick's from 1713 to his death in 1745. Best known as the author of *Gulliver's Travels,* that matchless satire on the rulers and the ruled, Swift used his slashing pen like a rapier and a rallying point against England in defense of Ireland, "an oppressed, insulated, and plundered nation," in the words of his admirer Wolfe Tone.

An eccentric and brilliant man unable to move upward in the church because of his attacks on England, Dean Swift was much loved by his fellow Dubliners, and there must have been a great deal of talk about him in the pubs. Clearly a passionate man, his life provided excellent grist for the gossip mills. He was closely associated with a woman named Esther Johnson, whom he called Stella, and it is still not certain whether they ever married. According to some sources, they were cousins, both illegitimate children of the powerful Temple family, and therefore could never marry each other.

In the south aisle of the cathedral, opposite the second free-standing pillar, two bronze plaques mark the graves of Swift and Stella. Subsequent deans have moved poor Stella's body next to Swift's, or away from it, depending on whether they believed in the marriage theory or not. Ironically, this shunting about of the unfortunate remains is exactly the type of absurdity that would have earned an immediate jab from the Swiftian needle.

By the vestry room is the world's most famous epitaph, composed by Swift himself and translated from the Latin by Yeats:

> Swift has sailed into his rest,
> Savage indignation there
> Cannot lacerate his breast.
> Imitate him if you dare,
> World-besotted traveller; he
> Served human liberty.

DUBLIN CASTLE

The castle has contributed famous and infamous history to Ireland. The castle yard was once known as the Devil's Half-Acre. Over the gate the bronze figure of Justice holds her scales. Formerly, when the scales filled with rain, they would tip to one side, not a very auspicious sight for the local populace, so the embarrassed authorities drilled tiny holes to allow the water to drain.

Irish writer Sean O'Faolain defines the role of the castle in his country's history: "Dublin Castle had become the center of a softly purring machinery. It was to remain so until 1916. Unable to rule directly, the middle classes and gentry now had to persuade, influence, calm, and coax the native millions, and if necessary, to buy and bribe them with offices, jobs, favours, honours and above all by pure undiluted snobbery. With a minute garrison of British troops and a large *native* police force, the Castle did its job beautifully. Dublin's men of property, persuaded or purchased, bamboozled or bullied, played ball almost to a man. It was one of the nicest examples in history of quiet colonial rule by use of the kid glove and the tinkling purse."

An amusing footnote is that Bram Stoker, author of *Dracula,* a Dublin man, worked here as a clerk for ten years. It makes you wonder what happened in the castle when the moon was full.

Open to the public, the castle is still used for state occasions. Until recently Bedford Tower was used to house genealogical records.

MADIGAN'S
1 Moore Street

The perfect watering spot after a walk down crowded Moore Street among the stalls of Dublin's colorful open-air fish, vegetable, fruit, and clothing market, which is a great place for seeing Dublin faces and hearing English in a variety of accents. Wander among housewives with baby carriages, dogs, hawkers, and bargain hunters of all kinds.

Madigan's is a bit shabby and dark, but you'll enjoy the old photographs on the walls and the bustle of street vendors and their customers who come in for refreshment.

Entry into the European Common Market has opened the door of a highly critical and exacting market to Irish food producers . . . Irish meat, fish, dairy products and other processed goods are not only accepted but sought after in France, Germany, Holland, Belgium . . . Irish food products are exported to all five continents—pork to Japan, dairy products to Latin America and China, jam and marmalade to Middle Eastern countries, confectionary to Australia, mackerel to Nigeria and Jamaica; sea urchins, oysters, scallops and mussels to France; bacon to North America, duckling and chickens to Germany, herrings to Norway, cake to Kuwait . . . the list is endless.

Meat from Ireland—beef, pork, lamb and ham has a disease-free veterinary record unrivalled in Europe and an enviable reputation for quality.

—Rose Mary Craig
"Inside Ireland"

MADIGAN'S
Morehampton Road
Donnybrook
Food: Pub grub
This is the haunt of Dublin's radio and TV personnel. RTE (pronounced *oar-tee-ee*), Radio Telefis Eireann is an easy amble away. Writers and poets, painters, talkers, and would-be's also make this their headquarters.

The crack starts at lunch, and often the same crowd continues till evening, warming to a white heat of wit as the pints flow on. Every now and then someone will disappear for an hour or two to do a broadcast.

I was adopted by a group of habitués for an afternoon, and it took me a day to recover. Actually, perhaps I never will.

Madigan's is the sort of place you would call roomy, a big lounge with comfortable, nondescript seating and many seductive nooks. Upstairs is television, with a kind of desultory atmosphere.

McDAID'S
3 Harry Street

Haggard and thin they
stagger in.
Fat and stout they
waddle out.

Say McDaid's and people will answer Brendan Behan. Although the roistering writer is associated with practically every pub in Dublin, it is in a corner of McDaid's that he made himself at home with glass and typewriter.

This dark, ornate bar, with its high, well-smoked ceilings, has been a special port of call for writers, artists, and would-be literati for lo! these 120 years. On a good evening you could have been entertained by Behan, Patrick Kavanagh, and Flann O'Brien, any one of whom would have been enough. Present-day frequenters appear in garb and hairstyle of every sort, and while the interested listener can still hear some mind-boggling exchanges, there's also a lot of chatter that just passes for wit.

All three of the above-mentioned writers stayed true to the Dublin code that holds public drinking to be somehow essential to the writer's craft, and all three died in the 1960s of alcoholism. Young writers have a hard act to follow in more ways than one in Dublin, the city of writers.

Flann O'Brien is finally receiving the international attention he deserves. That he was difficult to discover may be due in part to his having carved himself into three people, all of whom he used, when necessary, as shields. As Flann O'Brien he wrote several novels that for their exuberant prose and sparkling invention have been proclaimed among the finest of the modern period; as Myles na Gopaleen (Myles of the Little Ponies) he wrote for twenty-five years a wildly imaginative newspaper column for the conservative *Irish Times;* as Brian O'Nolan, the name on his birth certificate, he held down a responsible job in the bureaucracy of the Irish government.

Dressed in his black hat, he was a true Dublin character, a loved and feared member of the pub circuit. His utterances were eviscerating yet playful, his ear for the humorous utterly accurate, his commitment to language true yet earthy. Here is Flann on the death of a friend:

Behan, Master of Language

Oscar Wilde denounced fox-hunting as the pursuit of the uneatable by the unspeakable, and one may perhaps sadly echo the witticism by saying that Brendan Behan's death is the triumph over the irrepressible by the irreplaceable (and he would be the first to snigger at the eccentric staggering of that little bit of English).

But it is quite true that he will not be replaced, either in a hurry or at all. There has been no Irishman quite like him and his playwriting, which I personally found in parts crude and offensive as well as entertaining, was only a fraction of a peculiarly complicated personality. He was in fact much more a player than a play-write or, to use a Dublin saying, "He was as good as a play." He exuded good nature. He excelled in language and was a total master of bad language. That latter part of his achievement must remain unknown to the world at large but his personal associates will sorrowfully cherish the memory of it as something unique and occasionally frightening. I have personally never heard the like of it, and it could become enchanting when the glittering scurrilities changed with ease from native Dublinese to good Irish or bookity French.

JOHN MULLIGAN
8 Poolbeg Street

Licensed in 1782, this is one of the oldest pubs in Dublin, and well worth a visit. Its exterior sports some nice old lettering on the windows: WINE, WHISKEY, BONDER, SPIRITS, and over the door PUBLIC BAR. The pint here is known far and wide to be one of the best in Dublin and has been enjoyed by many famous names, among them John F. Kennedy, who stopped in for a drink back in 1945, when he was working for the Hearst newspapers.

As a matter of fact, Mulligan's has long been a favorite with journalists, who find its dark, simple recesses to their liking. You'll find students here, too.

Mulligan's is associated with the theater, its walls decorated with theatrical posters from the old Theatre Royal across the street.

There are three bars, and while the atmosphere is congenial, it is not overcrowded.

A wide variety of Dubliners seem to have a particular, almost reverential fondness for this pub. It is always referred to as "Oh, yes! Mulligan's of Poolbeg Street," to distinguish it from lesser Mulligans.

SEAN MURPHY'S
1 Powers Court

At the moment of writing, this is an "in" pub, fondly referred to as "Scruffy Murph's" and in the hard-to-find category. But looking for pubs in Dublin is a sport in itself, enabling you to traverse terrain off the beaten tourist track and giving you a chance to at least peek behind the Georgian façades.

Scruffy Murph's is situated incongruously between a housing facility for the elderly and a pick-up area for young prostitutes—no connection. Women walking along the appropriately named Mount Street toward the arch that leads to Powers Court should therefore not be surprised or perturbed at cars that slow down to reveal leering drivers with suggestive questions.

Mount Street marks the site of an amazing event in the annals of the 1916 Rising. At the canal bridge, which now sports the ladies of the evening, ten of Eamon De Valera's daring volunteers fought 800 En-

EMINENT LITERARY DUBLINERS

Jonathan Swift (1667–1745), patriot, pamphleteer, satirist (*Gulliver's Travels*, etc.)

Edmund Burke (1729–97), orator and political philosopher, champion of American liberties.

Richard Brinsley Sheridan (1751–1816), actor and dramatist (*The School for Scandal, The Rivals, The Duenna*, etc.)

Thomas Moore (1779–1852), poet and adapter of Irish traditional airs

William E. H. Lecky (1838–1903), historian

Oscar Wilde (1854–1900), poet, wit, dramatist (*The Importance of Being Earnest, The Ballad of Reading Gaol*, etc.)

George Bernard Shaw (1856–1950), wit, dramatist, Nobel Prize winner

William Butler Yeats (1865–1939), poet, dramatist, Nobel Prize winner

John Millington Synge (1871–1909), dramatist (*The Playboy of the Western World, Deirdre of the Sorrows*, etc.)

James Joyce (1882–1941), poet and writer (*Dubliners, Portrait of the Artist as a Young Man, Ulysses, Finnegan's Wake*, etc.)

James Stephens (1882–1950), poet, author (*The Crock of Gold*)

Sean O'Casey (1880–1964), dramatist (*The Plough and the Stars, Juno and the Paycock*, etc.)

glish soldiers marching from Dun Laoghaire to Dublin and cost the British 234 casualties.

Originally a workingmen's pub, Sean Murphy's is 200 years old; a big, bare sort of a place with an endless wooden bar that turns around a corner. The walls are covered with ads and postcards—Sean Murphy has received over 500 from friends the world over. He says his place is more of a club than a pub, and he does seem to know everyone—and they all seem to know each other. Taking part in the ritual pint-drinking is an odd blend of working people, rugby players, and the "beautiful people" of Dublin, in some cases quite literally so, as it is a hangout for models of both sexes.

Though it may take a while to establish a conversational beachhead here, don't be discouraged.

NEARY'S
1 Chatham Street
Specialties: Smoked salmon, oysters in season

While some pubs are hidden away, like The Stag's Head or Sean Murphy's, you'll have no problem locating Neary's. First, because it's so well known that you can ask anyone to direct you there; and second, because it's easily recognizable. On either side of the entrance are two unusual beacons—large, bronze arms that seem to spring out of the brick, their bronze hands holding aloft lamps. Inside is a decorous Edwardian interior, elegant with well-preserved shining brass, milky, globed gas lamps, and satiny mahogany. The feeling is rather like that of a good "club," a sense of tradition upheld to just this side of stuffiness.

Upstairs is a calm, pleasantly lit lounge, in contrast to the downstairs bar, which seems like a Victorian stage set filled with a "mod" cast. With the Gaiety Theatre literally at the back door, there is a good chance that many of the "cast" really *are* actors, or in any case, after-theater revelers.

Neary's has a distinguished past as host to a variety of figures in "arts and letters" and is still a favorite meeting place to start out on an evening's adventure.

Supporters of the women's movement must be warned: women are not served pints—it is considered undignified. A lady reports going in one evening and asking for a pint of lager. She was courteously informed, "We don't serve pints to females." "Females," she sneered, "it makes me sound like a prize bitch at the RDS [Royal Dublin Society, which sponsors horse and hunt events]." She then cannily ordered two glasses (half pints), but still the bartender remained politely obdurate. So she got stocious on whiskey in revenge.

Anyway, the fresh, unsmoked salmon with brown soda bread is famous and *very* good. And the place is never overcrowded.

O'DONOGHUE'S
15 Merrion Road
No rucksacks or sleeping bags allowed reads the notice at the door. This famous pub, just a few doors from St. Stephen's Green, is the mecca for traditional Irish music. It was the launching spot for The Dubliners, who still play there, as do Irish musicians both known and unknown.

At O'Donoghue's the music is impromptu and inspired, and there are often two sessions going on at once: one in the front room, where the bar is, and another in the back room, where the salmon-colored walls are covered with photographs of musicians who have played there over the years.

The air is thick with smoke, smiles abound, and people move from the bar through the crowd juggling four and five pints for their friends.

The music is listened to with a light reverence that is very easy to fall into and the proceedings are aided by the atmosphere of an authentic old pub that has not been updated.

Come early on weekends if you want a seat.

THE OLD STAND
37 Exchequer Street
Specialty: Three-course hot lunch
The Old Stand is named after the old Rugby stand on Landsdowne Road, and it does attract the sporting crowd as well as students and business people. It's one of the few Dublin pubs to serve a hot lunch between 12:00 and 2:00 and a hot supper between 6:00 and 9:00. It's a good place to eat and drink before going to a sporting event.

There's something exceptionally cheerful about this pub, with its crisp red-and-white frontage and black-and-white interior. Perhaps it also has something to do with the big old stove that occupies the center of the bar, the carved shelving, and the shiny brass horse ornaments.

THE PALACE BAR
21 Fleet Street
This unspoiled pub is to be recommended for its delightful back room, where the lovely Dublin light streams down through a milky skylight, adding a special glow to the paintings, the old leather chairs, the faces of the drinkers.

Once the meeting place of writers and journalists, it's now very popular among the younger set of international tourists. I saw an old regular, with his *Irish Times* under his oxter, standing bewildered among the guitar cases and rucksacks.

THE PLOUGH
28 Lower Abbey Street

> *This is not, I say,*
> *The dead Ireland of my youth, but an Ireland*
> *The poets have imagined, terrible and gay.*
> —W. B. Yeats

The Plough is the place to have a drink either before, at the intermission of, or after attending the Abbey Theatre, which is across the street. Get into the mood here by looking at the old photos of Abbey performers and performances made famous long ago.

When you join an audience at the Abbey, Ireland's government-sponsored national theater, you are witnessing the culmination of much turbulent history. In the 1890s the long-suppressed grief and frustration of the Irish people found perfect expression in the words of her writers.

Led by William Butler Yeats, the Irish literary revival marked the rebirth of Irish pride in Irish identity, the same rebirth of pride that was to bring about the Irish Republic.

From the first, literature and politics existed in a relationship that was not merely intimate but incestuous. This new consciousness permeated most Irish literature of the time, but it was in the theater that it played its most important role as an arbiter of social change.

Before 1894 there had been many famous Irish playwrights: Congreve, Sheridan, Goldsmith, Wilde, Shaw; but while they were Irish in perception, they wrote in a British context. Then, in 1894, on a wet day in the Galway countryside, Yeats and Edward Martyn paid a historic call on Lady Gregory (see page 190) at her home in Coole Park. The trio discussed the need for an Irish theater, and the result was the Coole Manifesto:

> We propose to have performed in Dublin, in the spring of every year, certain Celtic and Irish plays, which, whatever be their degree of excellence, will be written with a high ambition, and so build up a Celtic and Irish

school of dramatic literature. . . .We will show that Ireland is not the
home of buffoonery and of easy sentiment, as it has been represented, but
the home of an ancient idealism. We are confident of the support of all
Irish people, who are weary of misrepresentation, in carrying out a work
that is outside of all the political questions that divide us.

From this beginning was born the Abbey Theatre, that group of actors and writers who were to change Ireland's destiny.

The most famous playwrights of the Abbey were, besides Yeats, John
Millington Synge and Sean O'Casey. Synge gave passionate voice to
the people of the country and O'Casey quick tongue to the lives of the
town. The Plough is named after O'Casey's great classic *The Plough and
the Stars*. In 1907, Synge's play *The Playboy of the Western World* precip-
itated a week of fighting both inside the theater and outside in the
streets. The rioting took place because Synge allowed one of his characters, a twenty-one-year-old Irish girl, to mention a "feminine undergar-
ment."

"In those days," reminisces an old actor, "the company could afford
only half a dozen full-time actors. Barry Fitzgerald and I were part-
timers. We were civil servants, actually. We'd work for the government
all morning, then rush to the theater at lunchtime to rehearse. Back at
our offices again by two, and to the Abbey at five for more rehearsals
and our only meal of the day. Then we'd start the performance at eight.
It was a kind of lunacy, but we did it because we loved the theater."

In 1951, the building housing the Abbey, sometimes called "the
Shabby," burned down. Members of the Abbey exulted as flames took
the building. Now the government would have to give them a new
home. The government did—but in typical Irish fashion, it took fifteen
years.

These days, the new $2½ million theater is filled to capacity more
often than not, and you can enjoy not only the playwrights of the Irish
revival but Behan, Joyce, and Shaw.

RYAN'S
28 Parkgate Street
Ryan's is a favorite of mine. A beautiful, tranquil jewel of a pub, metic-
ulously maintained and totally untouched by the renovators. The bar

takes up the center of the entire room, rather like a sleek mahogany ship lying at berth. The lighting is warmly dim; the ceiling is very high and crowned with a smoky, mirrored skylight.

The courtly old bartender wields a special power: he controls the latch to the snug, so that you can enter or leave only at his discretion. When you've finished with your tête-à-tête, you ring a little bell and he appears at the serving window to release you. So if you want to be captivated in more ways than one, Ryan's is your spot.

Ryan's also sports one of the most elegant bathrooms (or jacks, as they call it in Ireland) in town. Even the toilet is vintage polished mahogany.

SEARSON'S
33 South Richmond Street

Searson's is well over a hundred years old. The pub was formerly a Georgian house and was first opened in 1806. At the moment of writing it is a fashionable pub, but since the "trendy" crowd is fickle, it may not be by the time you read this.

The two downstairs bars are in the traditional Irish style. The upstairs lounge bar, which opens at 7:30 p.m., has a lovely open fire. The lounge windows offer a wide view of the canal and approach roads, which was why the rebels of the Easter uprising used this pub as a command post.

In the downstairs wine shop you can see mute testimony to the battles in the old bullet marks that scar the wooden beams.

THE STAG'S HEAD PUB
1 Dame Court

Music: Traditional—Tuesday and Friday nights at 8:30
Food: Fine pub grub, exceptional menu, whiskey and wine bottled on premises

Part of the fun of going to The Stag's Head Pub is finding it, hidden away as it is in the heart of the city center. (By the way, the words "AN LAR" that you keep seeing on those double-decker buses are Irish for city center.) Walk up Dame Street, Dublin's principal commercial and insurance street, keeping alert for a passageway marked in the pavement by a mosaic image of an elk. Duck through to cobblestoned Dame Court, where you'll discover a red-brick Victorian building complete

with bottle-glass windows and scrolly doorway. It looks very much the
tavern of old etchings, as well it might; it has remained unchanged
since it began serving Dubliners in 1890.

Inside is a delightfully warm atmosphere, all old leather and polished
wood. The original stained-glass windows shed a gentle light, each
sporting a stag's head in the center of a leafy scroll. Along the right wall
runs a mahogany bar topped with a counter of red Connemara marble.
Above the bar, mildly surveying his domain, is the proud namesake of
the place—a seven-point stag's head.

One of the main attractions of this pub is the excellence of its menu,
chalked up daily for the crowds of lunchtime habitués who flood in
from the surrounding offices and from the nearby Dublin Stock Exchange. (A *tip*: if you're lunching, get there either before the big press,
about 12:00, or as it is clearing, about 2:00; otherwise you'll have a long
wait.) It's hard to choose among the array of Dublin specialities: the
joint-of-meat, steak and kidney pie, boiled bacon and cabbage, lamb
chops and stew. Each entrée is served with fresh soda bread.

Tuesday and Friday nights, go downstairs for a rousing evening of traditional and not-so-traditional balladeering. You will find that the
crowd is refreshing, only a smattering of tourists among a large number
of Irish young people who know most of the songs and who sing along
in high good humor. The atmosphere is spirited (pun intended), with
the audience and entertainers exchanging jokes and friendly gibes. Everyone talks to everyone, and you might even be invited home to a further singsong. Don't forget to sing even if you don't know the words.
Here is a song they might play:

Bottles of Black Porter

I was born so small and weak [wake]
No bottle could I touch or take
until the nurse the order spake,
'Go get that child some porter.'

And so to man's estate I grew.
My medicine chart no bottles knew,
No potions, pills, or powders blue
But bottles of plain porter.

Some fear to swim the River Lee,
The Shannon, Boyle or old Liffey;
But who wouldn't chance the Irish Sea
If frothy brine were porter?

Paddy Flaherty on a skite [binge]
Travelled pubs by day and night,
But what did he drink when he got tight?
He called for pints of porter.

And now my song has come to an end.
My homeward way I soon must wend.
I'm hoping that the gods will send
Another round of porter.

Chorus:
Tooriloo, riloo, riloo.
Tooriloo, riloo, riloo.
Tooriloo, riloo, riloo.
Oh give that child some porter.

TOM RYAN'S "51" CLUB
51 Haddington Road
Specialty: Cornish pasties

This pub may be called Tom Ryan's, but that's past history. Manager-owner Frank Taylor has made the "Club" his creation and very much a gathering place of the present. In a series of profiles on pub owners, *Business & Finance Magazine* drew a good portrait of the "51."

It is 5:30 on a Friday evening and the atmosphere in Frank Taylor's "51" pub in Haddington Road is getting extravagantly trendier. Dublin's advertising males and females eye one another, business types put down their briefcases and see who's wandering around, the vast banks and insurance blocks and semi-state bodies send envoys to the gathering and pretty soon everybody is crushed together, eating cocktail sausages, drinking "51" Specials and getting to know one another.

Frank Taylor watches it all inscrutably from behind his glasses and says: "A good pub owner is like the wise monkey—he sees, hears, and speaks no evil."

He is an interesting example of the Dublin publican. Despite a family tradition of publicans, Frank's father forsook the trade for life as a farmer, and Frank spent sixteen of his thirty-seven years farming in the North County–Dublin area. Though he still considers himself more a farmer than a publican, he was always intrigued with the idea of running a good pub. So he finally decided to call his own bluff. In 1975 he bought Tom Ryan's.

He set about remodeling the place, with the idea of creating "a pub that was as far away from Formica as possible." The result: subdued plush, brass and soft brown upholstery. He says there is a fair profit in the pub business but not what the public thinks. In addition to the overhead and taxes, there is also a mixture of dedication, work, and flair necessary to make a place successful.

He thinks good service is the most important thing in a pub; but though he doesn't see himself as "mine host" he thinks personalized service is important.

If you want to spend lunch observing Dublin interoffice intrigue, the "51" draws a big noontime crowd, and the food is good enough to have earned a distinction in the Tourist Board's National Bar Food Competition. You can get the American classic BLT (bacon, lettuce, and tomato), a great favorite with the Dubliners, as well as homemade Cornish pasties, and fresh soups.

With the usual turnover for this sort of pub, it may be that Frank Taylor, restless for new challenge, has already sold it to begin again somewhere else.

A cardinal Irish rule is that what is said when drink is taken is never repeated the next day or held against you. In fact, even in court, the best defense the accused can offer is, 'Drink was taken'. That plea will always soften the verdict from an Irish judge and jury.

—John McCarthy
Ireland of the Welcomes

TONER'S
139 Lower Baggot Street
Toner's is truly a pub of character. Look up at the wonderful carvings at the corner of the building as you enter.

Behind the bar you can see the timeless reflection of merrymakers in the dim mirrors. The old mahogany storage drawers for tea form a colorful feature of the decor, as does the perfect little snug to the left of the door, usually crammed full.

It is one of the few remaining Dublin pubs that serve whiskey from the cask, and it also is one of the few pubs to have been visited by W. B. Yeats.

DALKEY

Dalkey, a fashionable suburb of Dublin, is a picturesque village about eight miles from Dublin's center. It can be reached easily by train or bus. If you're driving, you'll be taking the beautiful "Rocky Road to Dublin" celebrated in the song.

THE QUEEN'S
Castle Road
Food: Soups, grills, salads, sandwiches, desserts
The Queen's is elaborately modernized in nautical-cum-tavern style, with plenty of ship's artifacts, pewter tankards, leaded windowpanes, and comfortable seating.

The Queen's is one of the oldest taverns in Ireland, receiving its first license in 1779, and naturally the premises are imbued with historical lore. The nautical theme of the tavern is no accident: Dalkey was built on shipping. In the time between 1200 and 1600, Dalkey was *the* port of all Ireland, the landing point for all merchant shipping. There is a fine view of Dublin Bay from Sorrento Park and Sorrento Terrace.
Required reading: The Dalkey Archives, a novel by Flann O'Brien.

THE CLUB
Ten miles from Dublin, this pub has had the honor of winning the Best Dublin Pub award three years in a row. Its fame has meant that at night

it is nearly always jammed (forget weekends unless you are partial to crowd scenes), but at lunchtime or in the afternoon it is pleasant. Hugh Leonard, columnist and author of twenty-one plays including *Da*, winner of a Tony Award, the New York Critics Circle Award, and numerous other citations, who claims The Club as his local, says, "The pub grub is first-rate, and the owner, Seamus Sheeran, happily acts as postmaster, moneylender, casher of checks, and general amanuensis for his regulars."

CITIES OF THE FIELDS

The fact that we survived as we did and are still one of the most rooted peoples in western Europe is a tribute to our doing things in a rather wayward uncentralised fashion many tidy-minded people don't approve of. The hundred-odd kings of early Ireland were each monarch of his own little territory or *tuath*, each often quarrelling with or raiding his neighbours. But whatever culture these chieftains shared together must have been much stronger and more enduring than what divided them. A great historian of early Ireland has written of their little kingdoms:

> We find the ancient Greeks organised like the Irish in small political communities, but these communities under the influence of the older Mediterranean civilisations and commercial life are based in each case on a walled town. The Irish remained a rural city, a city of the fields.

"A city of the fields": this gives the clue to its strength. A rural city which is part of a larger culture but is politically autonomous can command great loyalty and devotion. The Irish system of decentralisation and loyalty to a locality has endured.   —Séan O'Tuoma

COUNTY WICKLOW

> There is a primal quality to this country, the landscape has a wildness. The light is almost magical, though it does change a lot. . . .It is said you can have all four seasons in one day and I've known it to happen more than once these past couple of months.
>
> —John Boorman, film director, on shooting
> *Excalibur* at the National Film Studios in Wicklow

"There's gold in them thar hills." This time the rush was made up of writers rather than miners, the motivation tax exemption instead of gold nuggets, and the hills those of Wicklow rather than California.

In 1969 Charles Haughey, then Finance Minister, introduced the Finance Act, which removed taxation from certain types of creative work. The result of this enlightened legislation was an immediate flow of artists and writers into Ireland. Ten years later, English writer Neil Boyd explained: "I would never have left England voluntarily, but the fact is that had I remained in England paying 83% tax, I couldn't guarantee that I could afford to be a writer in even three years' time. The Irish government have sensibly recognized that, without a degree of financial security, a writer cannot continue to write."

Writers coming from countries in the European Economic Community benefit more, since they pay no tax in their own country. American writers have to pay taxes at home, though at a reduced rate, and Irish writers can now stay happily (at least tax-wise) at home.

The domed hills of Wicklow, with their own special wild beauty, are yet only twenty miles from Dublin. Wicklow is the perfect location for a writer. Here is the healing solitude and the benign detachment of nature within easy reach of the business contacts and hum of the city. Writer and journalist Hugh Leonard, who makes his home in Dalkey, sees a bit of a dark lining to the silver cloud, however:

> The writers who come here to live tend to buy large houses surrounded by high walls and expect the community to come in, rather than going out and mixing with them.
>
> Some people can't take life here. We're rather sloppy and don't tend to

do jobs well or thoroughly. And, in Ireland, everyone will know your business—It's not a good place to have a mistress. It's a very slow-moving country, but the nice thing about living in it is that you can make your own pace while other people can live either faster or slower as they wish. A Spaniard once asked for the Irish equivalent for the word mañana. He was told that there was no word in the Irish language that conveyed the same sense of urgency.

The writers of the present day who are hiding out in Wicklow are following in the footsteps of one of Ireland's greatest writers—John Millington Synge, who in a wilder day wandered Wicklow and made of the mountains his hermitage and inspiration. The following is taken from *The Complete Works of J. M. Synge*:

> *Still South I went, and West and South again,*
> *Through Wicklow from the morning to the night,*
> *And far from cities and the sights of men,*
> *Lived with the sunshine and the moon's delight.*
> *I knew the stars, the flowers and the birds,*
> *The grey and wintry sides of many glens,*
> *And did but half-remember human words*
> *In converse with the mountains, moors and fens.*

Synge belonged to the tradition of writers who view life as a journey and who translate this perception into a deep love for the open road. Jack Butler Yeats remembered Synge as "an old dog for a hard road and not a young pup for a tow-path. . . .He gathered about him very little gear, and cared nothing for comfort except perhaps that of a good turf fire."

It was not only the landscape of Wicklow that informed the heart and mind of Synge but the language and life of the people themselves. Like other writers of the Irish literary revival, Synge looked to the traditions and musical speech of the people of the land for his literary voice:

In writing *The Playboy of the Western World*, as in my other plays, I have used one or two words only that I have not heard among the country people of Ireland, or spoken in my own nursery before I could read the newspapers. . . .When I was writing *The Shadow of the Glen* . . . I got more aid than any learning could have given me from the chink in the floor of the old Wicklow house where I was staying, that let me hear what was being said by the servant girls in the kitchen."

Where the imagination of the people, and the language they use, is rich and living, it is possible for a writer to be rich and copious in his words, and at the same time to give the reality, which is the root of all poetry, in a comprehensive and natural form.

Nowadays, the romantic tramp life that brought Synge in touch with a special breed—those he termed the poets of the road—has largely disappeared from Wicklow. Northeast Wicklow is anglicized, polite, and tidy, and the pretty villages are part of the tourist route. But secondary roads leading off into the heather still abound in untrammeled beauty, and nothing can dim the allure of the land itself.

GLENDALOUGH

Many of the nobles of the English nation and lesser men also had set out thither, forsaking their native island either for the grace of sacred learning or a more austere life. And some of them indeed soon dedicated themselves faithfully to the monastic life, others rejoiced rather to give themselves to learning, going about from one master's cell to another. All these the Irish willingly received, and saw to it to supply them with food day by day without cost, and books for their studies, and teaching, free of charge.

—The Venerable Bede

Take what is known as the Military Road rising dramatically into the hills over Sally Gap to Glendalough. The name of the road survives from 1798, when it was built in an effort to root out the rebels who had taken refuge in the sanctuary of the mountains.

Follow the road through Ballyboden and then to the right and left as it winds to the summit of Featherbed Mountain. There's a grand view of Dublin Bay from the top, where the road levels out to reveal the Wicklow Mountains spread before you.

En route to the summit is the roadway leading to the notorious eighteenth-century club known as the Hellfire Club. Take the Forestry Department roadway to a point just above an old building that now houses the Hellfire Art Gallery and you'll find the abandoned ruin of the clubhouse looking properly evil and haunted.

The Hellfire Club was a scandalous rendezvous for the reckless young blades of the aristocracy. Here, in secret revolt against the strictures of religion and society, they staged wild bouts of gambling and drinking; and here, too, they abducted and raped rich young heiresses, compromising them into lucrative marriages.

As if these goings-on were not enough, local gossip has it that Black Masses were celebrated here. There is even a story that holds the Devil responsible for the eventual demise of the club. During a game of cards, a stranger joined the gambling. Someone chanced to look under the table, and lo and behold! there were cloven hoofs where feet should have been. Understandably, even the most outrageous of the members thought better of attending any further meetings and the place fell into disrepair.

Continuing southeast on the Military Road after this side adventure is like going from sinner to saint. Glendalough, or Glen of the Two Lakes, is a mystical valley bathed in a light so rare and kind that it is no wonder a saint chose this spot for his hermitage.

St. Kevin came here in the sixth century to meditate in radiant solitude, living as an anchorite and sleeping sometimes in the hollow of a tree. According to legend, he was forced to change his bed to a cave high in the cliffs above the upper lake because of the unwanted attentions of a lovely lady named Kathleen. Apparently, hearing him preach, she felt a great love for the handsome young monk rather different from the kind of love he was teaching. She courted him with a terrible persistence; not even his retreat to the cave discouraged her—she tracked him to his secret hideaway by following his dog. Awakening to find her bending over him must have been the final act that pushed him over the edge of sanity, which he manifested by pushing *her* over the edge of his cliffside perch to her death. Apologists pooh-pooh this story, claiming the saint would never have committed such a sin; but haven't you personally known of occasions that were enough to drive even a saint to acts of temporary madness? Anyway, you can climb to the cave, the recesses of which are today covered with the initials of many pious and curious visitors, among them Sir Walter Scott.

After a time, Kevin attracted more appropriate companions in the persons of other like-minded souls, and gradually Glendalough, with Kevin as its seed and heart, became a monastic city and a great center of medieval learning, attracting the finest scholars from all over and disseminating knowledge to Britain and to the courts of the European kings.

The remarkable city thrived, endowed with gifts from near and far, and was therefore a lucrative target for the plundering attacks of the Danes, the Normans, and the Irish themselves. It finally fell to the forces of Richard II in the fourteenth century.

All that now remains is the wonderful light, seven remarkable early churches, an enchanted cemetery full of Celtic crosses, a round tower, the gates to the city, and many legends and stories, such as the one about St. Kevin praying with his arms outstretched for so long that a bird nested in one of his hands.

Glendalough was part of a monastic movement that took place from the fifth to the ninth centuries over all of Ireland, leaving behind the beehive dwellings, the oratories, the burial enclosures that we find so moving today. The monks not only introduced to Ireland the craft of writing and illuminating but preserved Latin culture at a time when the collapse of the Roman Empire was threatening its extinction. This is a case of historical irony, since the Roman legions never arrived in Ireland, and thus its Celtic heritage was preserved.

When you visit Glendalough, I suggest you try to make it either out of season or late in the evening so that you can avoid the transistor radios and the tours; however, even if that is not practical, you will find a unique tranquillity to this spot that somehow transcends even the most blatant onslaughts.

After Glendalough, proceed to Roundwood only a few miles away for the comforts of a truly picturesque village. The village green is much the same as when Synge photographed the markets and the fairs that took place there.

ROUNDWOOD

ROUNDWOOD INN
Food: Excellent pub grub
A truly authentic cottage, like Durty Nellie's (see page 156), but less

self-consciously antique, this pub is one of the nicer ones in Ireland. It is both a restaurant and a pub, popular as a Sunday-lunch stop with the Dublin crowd out for an afternoon in lovely surroundings.

The pub grub is first-rate here, with chicken-in-the-basket and smoked-salmon sandwiches a specialty. Dress is informal in the pub, but be forewarned—a jacket and tie are required in the dining room.

COUNTY WEXFORD

Each county in Ireland seems to have a personality all its own, a surprising fact in a country so small. The Gaels called Wexford For-Tuathe-Mara, the land of the strangers by the sea, and regarded this region as a place apart. And that is a feeling you still do receive from Wexford.

Carnsore Point, the southeast corner of Ireland, was once thought of as a demon-possessed spot because so many sailors went to their deaths in the perilous currents and drifts formed as the waters of the Atlantic met the Irish Sea. Ptolemy, the second-century A.D. Egyptian mapmaker, knew Carnsore Point as Hieron Akron—the Sacred Promontory—a place of Druidic rites. A few years ago it was in the news as the site of a large antinuclear demonstration.

The people of Wexford, a mélange of Gaelic, Norse, Norman, Flemish, Welsh, and English ancestry, hold in common a particular memory that will not be forgotten—they are still haunted by the uprising of 1798. So dedicated was Wexford to this rebellion and so terrible was the retribution when it failed that the scars are felt today and the heroes still celebrated.

WEXFORD

From the dim times of antiquity the town of Wexford has looked out beyond the seas. Its origins are mysterious, but stone axes and artifacts reveal that organized communities thrived around 2000 B.C., and over the years this town on the Slaney River has become an international marketplace, a bazaar, and a busy port.

Today's narrow, winding streets, the successors of the ninth-century market trails, are much the same as they were in the tragic time of the '98 rebellion—lined with houses and shopfronts with curlicued old signs. The modern affliction of traffic jams seems oddly out of place.

Wexford is the home of an established artistic event of international significance—the widely acclaimed Wexford Opera Festival. The policy of the festival organizers is to produce rarely performed works with the best musicians, singers, conductors, and producers available. In October, critics, talent scouts, socialites, and opera lovers from all over make their way to Wexford. The festival is unique. The townspeople join in year after year to make the scenery and costumes, and to form the excellent chorus (all on a voluntary basis), as well as to perform the myriad organizational tasks that ensure a success.

The festival has, of course, spawned side events: flower and art shows, revues, lectures, walking tours. My favorite is the window-display competition, in which the various butchers, grocers, and bakers go to wonderful lengths to capture the prize.

If you tire of town, there are fine beaches nearby; if you enjoy spectacular gardens, try Johnstown Castle between Rosslare and Wexford.

THE CROWN
Monks Street

The Crown is just around the corner from Wexford's most fashionable hotel, White's. It was established in 1841 as a stagecoach inn. The Crown is distinguished by a fine collection of guns, among them the one used by the famous patriot Michael Collins (see page 150).

THE CAPE OF GOOD HOPE
North Main Street

Con Macken is the proprietor here, and he is famous as the uncle of Eddie Macken, the international horse-show jumping champion. His pub is one of Wexford's oldest, situated alongside the quay, where the shallow-bottomed boats draw up for the marketplace.

Con Macken provides all you'll ever need in this life, and even beyond: he runs one of the last pubs in Ireland to combine the services of a grocery store, a pub, and an undertaker. It's practically unnecessary to leave the premises until you go feet first.

COUNTY WESTMEATH

The heart of the midlands, Westmeath is the land of meadows and lakes, of myth and story.

ATHLONE

Athlone is really the central city of the midlands, at what some Irish wags refer to as "the dead center of Ireland." It is situated on the Shannon River and is an excellent center for exploring the shores and islands of Lough Ree. This lake, meeting place of three counties, Westmeath, Roscommon, and Longford, is really not a lake at all but the enlarged bed of the river Shannon. Several of its many islands harbor the skeletons of ruined churches on their woodsy shores.

There is not a great deal to say about Athlone except that it has a pretty marina and a lovely river park with cascades of sky-tinted water to please the eye and heart.

Fourteen miles east of Athlone on the Mullingar road is the place traditionally known as the true "center of Ireland," the Hill of Uisneach. Uisneach has been described as the navel of Ireland, and it is no ordinary mound; physically its slopes stretch out over five townlands and historically over many centuries, back into prehistory. Earthworks, ring forts, stones, and tumuli are scattered over its surface, creating a deserted village of the ancients.

On the southwest slope is a large natural rock formation called the Catstone because it crouches like a cat watching a mouse. The ancient tribes called it "the rock of the Divisions" because it marked the midland boundaries of the five original provinces:

> The nobles of Ireland came to accompany Fintan to Uisneach and they took leave of one another on the summit. And he set up in their presence a pillar-stone of five ridges exactly on top of Uisneach. And he assigned a ridge of it to every Fifth in Ireland, for Tara and Uisneach are in Ireland as two kidneys in a beast. And he marked out a *forrach* there, that is, a portion of each Fifth in Uisneach. (from an ancient manuscript)

In later times St. Patrick made his bed upon Uisneach, and St. Brig-
id is said to have professed her religion here. She is commemorated by a
shrine and a holy well.

Here, too, was the home of the three bright Sons of Uisneach, who
figure in *The Sorrowful Death of the Sons of Uisneach*, one of the Ulster
Cycle of Celtic tales. As the story unfolds, Niasi, one of the sons,
elopes with Deirdre (of the Sorrows), provoking the wrath of her be-
trothed, the aging High King Conchbar, who retaliates by killing the
Sons of Uisneach.

SEAN'S
King's Road

Tucked in a narrow street, Sean's is the type of tavern you probably
imagined as the typical Irish pub when you bought this book. It is long
and narrow, with small, scarred wooden tables and a fireplace around
which gather the usual assortment of Irish local people. The ceilings are
low, the walls smoky, the windows small and dim. When I asked the
age of the place, I was told, "Oh, sure, and 'tis very old."

On the wall opposite the bar, preserved under a dusty pane of glass, is
a bit of wall from a crannog house, the ancient, wattle lake dwellings
that housed the ancestors of those drinking here.

At any time in Sean's someone is likely to break out a guitar and/or
other instrument and perform a variety of ballads from traditional to
rock, from Kevin Barry to Eric Clapton. (I once saw graffiti on an Irish
wall that said *Clapton is God.*) The mood at Sean's is cozy and communal; indeed, it is a kind of clubhouse for the young of Athlone and the
farms around it.

Once Ireland's greatest export, the young are now leaving the country only as tourists, visiting Spain and Africa, Britain and Europe, but
returning home to tell of their travels. The job search here is a problem
for the young, as it is all over the world, but that was not the major
reason for present-day emigration.

Those who do leave now are escaping rather than fleeing. A twenty-
year-old friend of mine from Athlone left for New York because she
found Irish life too cramped and the future too lacking in imaginative
potential.

Sitting over a pint in Sean's one month before leaving, she explained, "The worst is that you've no life of your own. Everyone knows every move you make here. Attitudes are totally conventional and materialistic."

She wants to break away from the life style ruled by family, clan, and local loyalty, by obligation, by the preordained patterns of early marriage, children, and bourgeois values.

Yet the old rhythms are deeply ingrained. Six months later in New York, she is still somewhat reluctant to experience life outside the shelter of the Irish community. She calls home periodically to touch base. She will not return to that smothering life, she says firmly, but there is something wistful in her voice.

A wild youth, wayward but full of tenderness and affection, quits the country village where his boyhood has been passed in happy musing, in idle shelter, in fond longing to see the great world out of doors, and achieve name and fortune—and after years of dire struggle and neglect, and poverty, his heart turning back fondly to his native place, as it had longed eagerly for change when sheltered there, he writes a book and a poem, full of the recollections and feelings of home—he paints the friends and scenes of his youth, and peoples Auburn and Wakefield with remembrances of Lissoy.

—William Makepeace Thackeray
Oliver Goldsmith

LISSOY

Bordering Lough Ree, nine miles north of Athlone, is Oliver Goldsmith country. The eighteenth-century poet and writer, author of *She Stoops to Conquer*, was raised in the little town of Lissoy, or Auburn, made famous by his poem "The Deserted Village."

> . . . *Sweet smiling village, loveliest of the lawn,*
> *Thy sports are fled, and all thy charms withdrawn;*
> *Amidst thy bowers the tyrant's hand is seen,*
> *And desolation saddens all thy green:*
> *One only master grasps the whole domain,*
> *And half a tillage stints thy smiling plain.* . . .

> Far, far away thy children leave the land.
>   Ill fares the land, to hastening ills a prey,
> Where wealth accumulates, and men decay;
> Princes and lords may flourish, or may fade;
> A breath can make them, as a breath has made:
> But a bold peasantry, their country's pride,
> When once destroyed, can never be supplied.

This poem was inspired by the Enclosure Acts, which drove the peasants off their lands; Lissoy has still not recovered.

THREE JOLLY PIGEONS

A true eighteenth-century alehouse, with the appropriate accoutrements and some good chat, not necessarily about Goldsmith.

COUNTY KILDARE

A television quizmaster asked a Kildare contestant if he knew the author of *Gone with the Wind*. "No, but I know who trained him," came the response.

This is your county if you are a horse lover. Kildare, an inland county, is famous as a sporting, racing, and hunting region, which is understandable as it is perfect land for such uses: lush green pastures, big open grasslands, and large tracts of ancient bogland are interspersed with trees and gently rolling hills.

Horses have been an integral part of Irish life for centuries, and Irishmen are skilled horse breeders and riders to the very marrow of their bones. The Irish thoroughbred and hunter are in demand the world over, and racing and hunting amount to a national passion that crosses all economic and class barriers. In Irish eyes, it is simply country living.

For a number of people, hunting and Ireland are virtually synonymous, and visitors arrive from far and wide to join in the sport. Different parts of Ireland offer different terrain. There are eighty-five recognized hunting packs in the country, and several county hunts

SOME NOTES ON SEX IN IRELAND

Advertisements by the Mercier Press, Irish publishers

The Chastitute
A Play by John B. Keane
A chastitute is a person without holy orders who has never lain down with a woman, a rustic celibate by force of circumstance peculiar to a countryside where the Catholic tradition of long-life sexual abstemiousness is encouraged and free-range sex is absolute taboo.

Sex Instruction for Irish Farmers
Charles McSherry
There is no reason why agricultural bachelors should not be a thing of the past if farmers follow the expert advice given here by McSherry. He shows the reader how to go out and find a mate; how to "prepare the soil"; how to sow the seeds of a fruitful relationship and how to reap the bounty from your labours. McSherry's book is a hilarious romp through Irish country life.

I have never held the view that the Catholic Church is busy with a huge stick, keeping the Irish in some state of servile terror. The Church is only the sum of what people think, priests and bishops have exactly as much power as the community gives them. . . . Women are not drummed out of small towns if they have an illegitimate child. . . . Anyone I know in Ireland who has an affair with someone married, or whose marriage has broken up, suffers the same pangs of unhappiness as anyone in any other part of the world. . . . People have to make arrangements which are just as painful as those made in countries where divorce is acceptable.

—Marianne Baker
Cosmopolitan

have been in existence for generations. Mastership of some of the hounds has remained in the same family for over a century, and many packs have preserved their original strain of hounds.

People addicted to the sport say there is nothing as exhilarating as riding over the dewy morning fields, clearing every sort of obstacle in a headlong rush of horse, hound, and rider. Not everyone, however, is so enthralled. (For information on how you may join a hunt, write to Inside Ireland, 46 Lower Baggot Street, Dublin 1, Ireland.)

Horses are especially dear to the hearts of the Irish, but they are big business, too. Most of the fashionable thoroughbred sires are owned or syndicated by the big stud farms at service fees beyond the means of the small breeders. To help the latter, the state maintains several high-class studs at the National Stud at Tully in Kildare. In other parts of the country, too, the state provides excellent thoroughbred, hunter-type, and draught sires for the benefit of the farmers in general.

On the western side of Droichead Nua on the Naas road is The Curragh, a vast, dramatic plain that has been a horse-racing venue for two thousand years and is still going strong. Its name is derived from the Irish word "curragh," meaning "race horse."

The Curragh is the headquarters for Irish racing today; here the Irish Derby and several other classic races are decided. There are thirty-one tracks in Ireland, and horse racing and breeding play a significant role in Ireland's social and economic life. The Curragh is the main training center, with upward of 500 horses being prepared there by over twenty trainers.

Many overseas enthusiasts, including a high proportion of rich Americans of Irish ancestry, race horses trained here. With these resources behind them, trainers have the means to obtain top quality at the world's major bloodstock auctions.

Note: A beautiful stop: the Japanese Gardens at the National Stud in Tully, which are laid out in traditional Japanese symbolic style: bonsai trees, wooden bridges, shrub-embowered statues, etc.

NAAS

Naas to me is always a milestone signifying that I am either on the final approach to Dublin or that I've left its direct sphere of influence. It also

means that I'm about to leave or enter a horrific traffic jam. In any case, The Five Lamps is a good place to stop and catch your breath, whatever the direction you're heading.

THE FIVE LAMPS
Food specialty: Homemade soup
A small, quiet, homey pub run impeccably by a mother and daughter. Don't leave without trying the homemade soup and the fresh sandwiches. The soup is special. As I was sitting and savoring a barley version, three children appeared breathlessly in front of the bar. They asked to go into the garden to get their ball, which had bounced over the fence by mistake.

Wonderful knickknacks abound, such as porcelain monkeys outrageously attired; and in the upstairs hall on the wall by the neat bathroom are framed covers of *Vanity Fair*.

ROBERTSTOWN

Crossing the river Liffey by an impressive aqueduct, you reach Robertstown, a canal-side village on the summit level of the Grand Canal, before it begins the descent to the Shannon Basin.

Conscious of the contribution the canal has made to their past, the townspeople have refurbished the old Canal Hotel as a museum, and you can enjoy an eighteenth-century candlelight banquet here during the summer months.

Robertstown has another claim to fame: it is the Falconry of Ireland, where a wide variety of hunting birds can be seen in action.

THE BARGE INN
Twilight is the ideal time to be in Robertstown if you can arrange it. Get a pint from the barman at The Barge Inn and sit on the canal wall. Soon you will feel you've entered a time warp and landed in the eighteenth century. The tranquillity is complete: swallows dart overhead, and across the canal hayricks sport their white protective kerchiefs. The air over the water is still and smells faintly of turf smoke; the only sounds are those of dogs, birds, and people from inside the pub.

The pub decor is that of the usual Irish country tavern, but drinking there may be some of the men who used to crew the commercial boats—known in Ireland as canal boats, not barges. Buy a round of Guinness (made from the soft water of the canal itself, suitably filtered, of course) and you might hear tales of the old days and nights spent traveling the canal.

KILCULLEN

This little town beside the Liffey is four miles south of Droichead Nua. Two miles south, at Old Kilcullen, are the remains of a round tower and three ninth-century high crosses (see page 239).

THE HIDEOUT
This pub is a large complex of rooms with dark wood walls, fireplaces, historical artifacts, stuffed animals, and fish gracing the walls and corners.

I would not have believed it had I not seen it with "me very own eyes," but a prized and truly unique artifact here is the entire arm, mummified and on display in a glass case, of the great Irish boxer Dan Donnelly. Go ahead, call me a liar—you won't be the only one—even natives had trouble with this one.

I was not informed as to how The Hideout came into possession of this portion of poor Donnelly's anatomy, but it does make for interesting speculation. Dan was a celebrated boxer, a giant among men. A few miles away, at Donnelly's Hollow at the eastern end of The Curragh, Donnelly fought a famous match in 1815 in which he defeated the English champion George Cooper. You can still see the outsize prints his feet made that day as he left the hollow. They have been retrodden into permanence by countless visitors since, perhaps in the hope of receiving osmotically some of the giant's prodigious strength.

ATHY

South on the Dublin-Waterford road is Kildare's largest town, Athy. Here the rich farmers and horse breeders come to do their business and marketing.

The town is guarded by White's Castle, overlooking the Barrow River. It was built in the sixteenth century by the Earl of Kildare.

JEAN-BAPTISTE MAHER
MORTICIAN AND PUBLICAN

I heard of this pub from a friend of mine who swears it's a nice place. He's an eccentric horse breeder devoted to women and vodka and given to wearing a rumpled tweed suit that looks as if it might also do as a nest for a family of birds.

There's a lot to say in favor of having your publican double as your future mortician—if you're friendly with him, you'll at least be assured that you will go to your just reward in one piece, avoiding the possibility of a fate like that of poor Dan Donnelly.

COUNTY KILKENNY

Kilkenny is a gently undulating county threaded with the rivers Nore and Barrow. In the north are the lovely uplands of the Castlecomber district, and in the west the Slieveardagh Hills and the Booley Hills extend across the border from Tipperary.

KILKENNY

Kilkenny is a good-size (15,000) town for Ireland, with a special personality all its own. A labyrinth of narrow medieval lanes wind through, around, and even under old stone buildings. History is important in Kilkenny, and so is Irish culture.

The Kilkenny Design Centre, established to raise the standards of Irish industrial design, is internationally famous.

You can see workers at their crafts in a number of other communal workshops in Ireland, but Kilkenny is the best-known and most prestigious. Ironically, many of these have been set up in the former stables and yard buildings of Irish stately homes and castles.

The Kilkenny Design Centre is housed in what were once the stables of Kilkenny Castle. The Centre is a government-supported body that was set up some time ago to act as a catalyst to update Irish design. It is a showcase for the best of Irish handcrafts, and here the shopper can glory in soft woolens, sweaters, jewelry, linens, porcelain, glassware, rugs, kitchenware, and even hand tools. Outstanding is the quality and design of the metalwork.

Kilkenny Castle, at the southeast end of the city, stands on high ground beside the river Nore. Behind the towering, crenellated walls of this thirteenth-century building are a cool green park to the south and a formal garden to the north. The castle was erected on the site of a fortress built by Strongbow, but today it looks more like a mansion. The restored rooms reflect the style and taste of its nineteenth-century occupant, the Marquess of Ormonde.

When you visit the castle, make sure to leave by the footpath in the castle grounds that leads down some stone stairs to a wooden gate in the wall. This gate opens onto Canal Walk, a lovely path that meanders for a long way along the river, past castle walls, and through pleasant woods.

As with most medieval cities, Kilkenny's focal point is the cathedral, which stands high on a hill, an ancient round tower beside it, a reminder of the saints and scholars of the sixth century who founded St. Canice's monastery.

In the twelfth century, the monastic city was transformed into a secular town by the Norman invasion, and it is the Norman temperament that survives in the clean, classic lines of the cathedral built by them in the thirteenth century and dedicated to St. Canice.

Cromwell, whose desecration and utter despoiling of the cathedral is still remembered as a fresh tragedy (in Ireland the past has a way of never becoming the past), stabled his horses here. The cathedral has since been restored and retains many extraordinary statues and intriguing floor slabs.

As always, the Irish cast their spell over their conquerors, and the Normans became "more Irish than the Irish." Even the infamous 1336 Statutes of Kilkenny, a Norman attempt to break the spell, making it illegal for Anglo-Normans to marry Irish women, to play Irish games, to entertain Irish poets, and to speak the Irish language, did not succeed. The natives were dispossessed of their town and forced to live outside the walls, but all these efforts at apartheid proved unenforceable.

Rothe House on Parliament Street, now the house of the Kilkenny Library and Museum, is a handsome relic of late Norman times, with its arched façade and cobblestone courtyard.

In August Kilkenny is given over to the Kilkenny Arts Festival for one week (music, art, and literature), in keeping with its ancient reputation as a scholars' town.

TYNAN'S BRIDGE HOUSE
St. John's Bridge

This is a pub you'll want to take home with you. Tynan's, just beside the Nore, was consistently recommended to me as one of Ireland's best. With its beautifully preserved appointments, it is, as Hugh Leonard says, "an antiquarian's delight."

Tynan's was a pharmacy and grocery store, and has been Michael Tynan's pub since 1919. In perfect rows of shiny wood behind the front bar are ranks of drawers marked CLOVES, CITRON, ALMONDS, RICE, SAGO. An iron rail remembers when it used to support flitches of bacon from its hooks, an intricate old clock chimes the hour, a two-hundred-year-old scale, with its wonderful little cup weights, stands on the bar; and all is lit nostalgically by old, globed gas lamps in perfect working order. All this and more . . . as the ads used to say.

I sat down at the central bar, a kind of island in the middle of the room, and ordered a Smithwick's ale. An elderly gentleman with a kindly, ruddy face was seated beside me. "Damned good choice," he commented. "The name's Walter Smithwick," he said, holding out his hand and enjoying my flabbergasted expression.

Smithwick's, it turns out, have been brewing in Kilkenny since 1710. The brewery is built on the site of a twelfth-century Franciscan monastery, whose Romanesque tower is now surrounded by loading docks, beer kegs, and trucks—quite an expansion of the bit of brewing done by the good brothers, its former occupants.

Mr. Smithwick kindly invited me to visit him for breakfast at Kilkreen Lodge, the Smithwick homestead for several centuries. I was pleased to hear that I was partaking of rashers and eggs under the same roof that had sheltered such distinguished visitors as William Congreve and Jonathan Swift. After coffee in the greenhouse, Mr. Smithwick took me for a tour of Kilkenny. I guess I just know how to pick my ale.

KYTELER'S INN
Kieran Street

This inn has proffered victuals and spirits for six hundred years. The ground floor has been unremarkably modernized, but down one flight of stairs is the thirteenth century. A deep-set window overlooks St. Cieran's well, which outdates even the inn itself; and the original stone pillars reach floor to ceiling in this shadowy, candlelit cellar, which hasn't changed much from the fourteenth century, when Dame Alice Kyteler made the tavern a place of merrymaking.

Apparently, Dame Alice was good at more than merrymaking—she was a banker and a moneylender and laid four husbands to rest in the Kilkenny graveyard—under what were supposedly suspicious circumstances. In 1324 she was tried for witchcraft and condemned to be burned at the stake. She and her disciples were accused of sacrificing black cocks to the Devil and of brewing foul mixtures of their entrails and mixing them with herbs, insects, the hair and nails of unbaptized children, and dead men (the husbands?).

Alice escaped to England, but her maid, Petronilla, was not so lucky, and was burned.

To commemorate this macabre history, there is usually quite a celebration at Kyteler's on Halloween.

The food in the restaurant is good.

COUNTY OFFALY

Near the center of Ireland, this county is mostly level plain and bog, except for the aptly named Slieve Bloom Mountains in the southeast, which are blanketed with heather and which reward the explorer with beautiful hidden valleys.

SHANNONBRIDGE

The little village of Shannonbridge is so called after a graceful bridge of sixteen arches that spans the river Shannon here.

Four miles north is Clonmacnoise, one of the most important historic sites in Ireland. St. Ciaran founded a monastery here in 548, which flourished much as Glendalough did (see page 79), to become one of the most famous monastic cities of its time. As with Glendalough, Clonmacnoise's prosperity attracted plunderers down the centuries, and the city was finally given the *coup de grace* by the infamous soldiers of Oliver Cromwell.

The ruins consist of a cathedral, eight churches, two round towers, thirty wonderfully sculpted high crosses, two hundred sepulchral slabs, and the remains of a castle.

Set in the middle of uneventful bogland, this Oxford of medieval Ireland, intellectual headquarters for much of Europe, must have been an amazing place. In the monastic cities, Celtic and Latin traditions converged. Monastic life corresponded closely to the family patterns and tribal structures of the old Celtic life, and the manuscripts the monks compiled were adorned with marvelous Celtic organic tendrils and swirls winding around the Christian stories. The monks themselves evangelized Germania, Scotland, France, and Italy, extending their influence even as far as Iceland and America.

MICHAEL KILLEEN'S

This general store *cum* pub has pints as "black as an informer's heart" and a lovely turf fire. Over the fireplace is a framed likeness of the village's native son, actor George Brent, sporting a sunny smile that could dispel the worst gloom of a rainy Irish day.

COUNTY LONGFORD

Another of the inland counties, Longford is a land of quiet farmlands, brown bogs, and an occasional low hill. Pleasant vistas of lakes and riv-

ers winding through the landscape remind you of the background in a
medieval Flemish painting.

Longford is a county rich in literary associations: Oliver Goldsmith,
Maria Edgeworth, John Keegan Casey, and Padraic Colum.

LONGFORD

EAMON FARRELL'S
This is a cozy pub; but the main reason for stopping here is not the
decor but the personality of Eamon Farrell, who sparkles and crackles
like a warming fire.

COUNTY MEATH

For centuries Royal Meath, together with Westmeath, was a separate
province ruled by kings of pagan and early Christian Ireland. The county is rich with history—it was here in the ninth century at Kells that
the *Book of Kells*, that great, glowing masterpiece of illuminated art,
was created by the hands of the monks at St. Colmcille's monastery.

BETTYSTOWN

McDONAGH'S
Meath has a short strip of coastline, a grand sweep of sandy beach with
the twin resorts of Laytown and Bettystown. It was on the sands of the
beach at Bettystown that the eighth-century marvel of goldsmithing,
the Tara Brooch, was found on an ordinary day in 1850.

McDonagh's is a good-old thatched pub with one end devoted to gro-
ceries.

COUNTY LOUTH

Louth is Ireland's smallest county, covering 317 square miles and running northward from the river Boyne to Carlingford Lough. It is fertile land with a coast of wide sandy bays and rocky headlands. In the north is the mountainous Cooley Peninsula famous as the setting for many ancient epic tales, especially the "Tain Bo Cuailgne" (the Cattle Raid of Cooley, see page 210).

CARLINGFORD

The town of Carlingford is on the southern shore of Carlingford Lough at the foot of Slieve Foye. The ubiquitous St. Patrick is said to have landed here on his return from Rome, harkening to a voice in a dream that bid him return to the land where once he tended sheep for a Druid master. Perhaps, like many of us, he merely heard the call of Ireland herself and found it irresistible.

At one time this strategic harbor (used to plunder the hinterlands by early Norse raiders) had no less than thirty-two castellated buildings defending it.

In today's Carlingford you can see the massive sixteenth-century ruin of King John's Castle, or the large square of Taaffe's Castle (near Newry Street), with its wonderful spiral staircase leading to the battlements. Nearby, forming an arch over the roadway, is the "Tholsel," originally a gate tower in the town walls and in the eighteenth century used as a jail.

THE HARBOR BAR
This is a very nice small pub full of character. It is owned by Mr. P. J. O'Hare, who keeps an open fire going in the pleasant little lounge decorated with pub mirrors and curios. The Harbor Inn also doubles as a small grocery shop.

MONASTERBOICE

In this secluded spot six miles northwest of Drogheda, St. Biuthe established a monastery, probably in the fifth century. The ruins are impressive and include a round tower with a door six feet above ground level. In the old days the monks used removable ladders to climb into their antitroop shelters, but today things are a bit easier—you can get up via a modern staircase. Monasterboice is also the site of one of Ireland's finest high crosses (seventeen feet tall), the surface of which writhes with sculpted figures and designs.

THE MONASTERBOICE INN
On the road between Drogheda and Dundalk
Food: Pub grub exceptionally good
A modern pub, but tasteful; busy, full of local business people enthusiastically enjoying themselves. You can get a good pub lunch here.

Point of interest: Six miles from Dundalk, at Ratheddy, is "Clochafermor" or "Cuchulainn's Stone." According to legend, the great hero Cuchulainn, when he was mortally wounded, threw away his sword and bound himself upright to this stone so that even in death he would face his enemies standing. Not until a bird perched on his shoulder were his adversaries certain of his death. A bog near the stone, known as "Lochen an Chlaiomh" (the Lakelet of the Sword), is said to be the site where the fallen warrior's sword fell after he cast it from him.

COUNTY LAOIS

From the plain that forms most of this county rise the Slieve Bloom Mountains in the northwest—a surprise to those who think of Laois mainly as a road connecting Dublin, Cork, and Limerick.

COOLRAIN

SHEEHAN'S
This old pub offers a log fire all year round and tables made of old tree trunks. At closing time, the proprietress does not stand on ceremony. Instead of the usual "Time, gentlemen, please," she chases her customers out with a broomstick, a process that works and appears to be enjoyed by all.

PORTLAOISE

EGAN'S
Portlaoise (pronounced Port Leesh) is the county town and a kind of checkpoint on the Dublin-Cork road. Egan's, a "new place," is a good stop for a bit of pub grub if you've been driving without sustenance for a while, coping with the Irish charioteers on the dual carriageway (highway). It's true, the Irish will even admit to it themselves: they are erratic drivers given to dangerous bursts of vehicular impatience that can leave you breathlessly clutching your steering wheel, filled with a new comprehension of the phrase "the luck of the Irish."

COUNTY CARLOW

Tiny Carlow is shaped like an upside-down triangle. Small as it is, it is good climbing country, offering a pleasant upland in the northwest part of the county.

CARLOW

Carlow, a little river town on the banks of the Barrow, was once a stronghold of the Anglo-Normans, and its history is made up of a continuous series of struggles for possession of it. Today's citizens go about the peaceful business of flour milling, malting, and tending to the sugar-beet factory.

Two miles east of Carlow in Browne's Hill demesne (an old word for estate) is a dolmen (see page 163) whose 100-ton capstone is the largest in Ireland.

THE PLOUGH
Tullow Street

The Plough was established in 1929. It has a nice cobbled courtyard and over the door a miniature silver plow. The atmosphere is good, and there's a snug for private quaffing.

NEWTOWN

MICHAEL SMITH'S

Six miles south of Athy is this unusual pub run by Michael Smith, the fourth generation to serve here as publican. The pub is on the one street of the tiny settlement of Newtown, opposite the church and churchyard.

The amazing centerpiece of the pub is a grand piano that Mr. Smith bought in Germany many years ago and that is now valued at £30,000. Each Saturday and Sunday the pub features a musical evening.

MUNSTER

County Waterford   County Limerick

County Cork   County Clare

County Kerry   County Tipperary

Most people, even the Irish themselves, will agree that for sheer spectacle the province of Munster is particularly blessed. The south and southwest regions are geologically a system of east-west foldings of old red sandstone with limestone valley beds. Rivers have cut deep gorges between the ridges in some spots, providing literally breathtaking views. The ridges pile up into mountains that reach their maximum height in County Kerry.

Kerry is justly famous for its fish-laden rivers, mysterious mountain lakes, and twisting, tortuous coastline. North of Kerry is Clare, with its eerie limestone desert, "the Burren," dotted with caves and sudden clear springs, and blooming with fauna found nowhere else in the world.

As you move south of Kerry to Cork, the land becomes more gentle, forming peaceful coves ideal for sailing and fishing. Here, the warming influence of the Gulf Stream turns Cork into the flowering Riviera of Ireland, complete with palm trees and many exotic tropical and semi-tropical plants.

To the north and east of Cork is County Waterford, which combines many kinds of beauty in its scenery, from the steep coast of sand-fringed bays to the hilly woods that border some of the finest riverland in Ireland. North of Waterford is Tipperary, Ireland's largest inland county, where losing yourself in the ferny mountain depths of the Glen of Aherlow is a must. The middle of the county is a broad plain through which flows the river Suir, and from this plain the rich land of the Golden Vale extends westward into County Limerick.

Much of County Limerick is low and undulating, particularly in the east. In the southeast, the Galtee Mountains spill over from Tipperary into Limerick. County Limerick is a place of quiet rural charm and offers some of the finest hunting country in Ireland.

COUNTY WATERFORD

WATERFORD

Beautifully situated on the river Suir, Waterford is one of Ireland's leading ports and harbors an enormous amount of container traffic to the southern United Kingdom and to the Continent. So it comes as no surprise to learn that Waterford is a commercial city. What is surprising is the nature of one of Waterford's largest businesses—education.

As a town of many schools, both day and boarding, Waterford's streets are filled with an unusually large percentage of young faces, their freshness forming an interesting contrast to the ancient walls, crumbling ruins, and storied past of this city.

And a colorful past it is, too. Like so many major Irish towns, Waterford became a point of contention as succeeding waves of outsiders attempted to subdue it. First came the inevitable Danes, who officially established the town in 835. In the eleventh century the power of the Danes was broken at the decisive Battle of Clontarf, where the legendary Irish leader Brian Boru won the battle but lost his life, a type of martyrdom that seems to be an Irish specialty.

In 1170, Diarmuid MacMurrough of Leinster invited the Anglo-Normans across the water to help him obtain the High Kingship, thus introducing the English to Irish soil and beginning the cycle of violence that was to last seven hundred years (and still continues in the North).

To cement the new union of forces, the Norman Earl of Pembroke, or Strongbow, as he is so romantically called, married MacMurrough's daughter Aoife in Reginald's Tower. This landmark built by the Danish is still visible in Waterford. It stands like a battle-scarred elephant at the edge of town. You can see the marks of history on its flanks or enter and enjoy the museum that has been established within it.

Throughout the Reformation, Waterford, while politically allied to England, resisted all blandishments and force and remained stubbornly Catholic, pledging allegiance to the Catholic kings. Waterford men even forced the notorious Cromwell to abandon his siege of the town; but finally, at the close of the seventeenth century, the city surrendered on honorable terms to William III.

It was in the eighteenth century that the city began to truly enjoy economic prosperity and from 1783 to 1851 produced the marvelous heavy glass that was to make Waterford's name famous around the world. Then, in 1851, as a result of the Great Famine and the ensuing depression that swept Ireland, the glassworks closed; for a century no one made so much as a drinking glass in Waterford.

In 1952, a new factory was opened; hand-blown and engraved Waterford is again pleasing the world market. On the average, the Waterford master blowers and engravers are probably the youngest in the world, having apprenticed in their craft at the age of fifteen. This happy state of affairs has meant that Waterford men no longer need to emigrate to seek their fortunes but can prosper at home.

Should you want to visit the glassworks, the excellent little magazine *Inside Ireland* can make the arrangements for you. Write to them at 46 Lower Baggot Street, Dublin.

Glass is for sale at Knox's and at Palmer's in Waterford, and a great example of old Waterford crystal is on display in the Chamber of the Public Library Building in the form of a magical chandelier.

THOMAS MAR
O'Connell Street

Thomas Mar is one of the last of a vanishing breed. He brews his own mix and bottles Guinness in his own bottles. His pub is "the real thing," a kind of "spit and sawdust" place full of character as well as characters. Hoist a jar here after buying some Waterford glass or on your way to the coast.

DUNMORE EAST

Nine miles southeast of Waterford city, at Waterford Harbour, the coastal town of Dunmore East perches on the tumbling cliffs above the bay. Below lie fine beaches and sheltered coves. In the nineteenth century, Dunmore East was a station for ships carrying mail between England and the south of Ireland; now it is a place to relax for the people of Waterford city, a summer resort, and an excellent spot to try your hand at angling.

THE STRAND INN

The Strand is a large, comfortable old place stretching lazily at the rim of the cliffs above the sea. It is a favorite spot for hoteliers. There are three rooms to entertain yourself in, plus a back room with a fish-netted ceiling, a plain but serviceable bar, and a variety of amusement machines.

The front room sports a small fireplace of stone and small tables. In the adjoining room is a long bar with a great deal of good-natured banter going on, and in the next room, benches and tables and excellent traditional Irish music.

THE BUTCHER

The Butcher is just what its name implies. It is housed in an old butcher shop, one half of which is still used for the purpose of selling meat. The place has been nicely refurbished in plain pine boards laid on the diagonal, and there is an attractive zinc-and-copper bar. The clientele are mainly young.

MAGGIE MAY'S

Strangers are seldom, in fact almost never, seen at Maggie's, and it is a place to go only if you have read the section in this book on deportment. It is, however, well worth a trip, and you'll find it a fascinating spot to sit and watch the action. The best way to describe it, besides calling it a local card players' hangout, is to tell you the story of my introduction to Maggie's and hope that you will pick up the flavor of this uniquely Irish place from my experience.

In the bar at the Strand Inn I became friendly with a Waterford man. After downing a truly impressive number of pints, he informed me in a confidential whisper that "ectually" he was secretary to the Taoiseach (the Prime Minister, pronounced approximately Teé shook. All efforts at pronouncing Gaelic are of necessity approximate). As we emerged, with a slight weave, from the heady atmosphere of the Strand, he pointed to a car in the parking lot and said solemnly, "Garda [police]. They always have to watch over me, you know, because of my job." He held up a finger and winked. I nodded conspiratorially, playing along.

We entered Maggie's cramped vestibule and encountered "herself" closeted behind a tiny counter surrounded by cigarettes and other paraphernalia for sale. Maggie, a shrewd-eyed, birdlike, elderly lady, greeted my companion perfunctorily and began quizzing me, gradually warming to a lively conversation about Dunmore East versus New York. All the while, though seemingly casual, she watched and listened to me very carefully.

Apparently I passed muster, because she called out, "Tom, here's someone come to see us from New York." Tom, a heavy-set middle-aged man I took to be her son, appeared, and after some pleasantries about the weather, he opened a door and motioned us into a large, smoky room full of simple tables, men in dark clothes, and pints. We chose a table and soon had our own pints before us.

The men in the room were playing a card game that required them to knock loudly on the table at certain intervals. The quiet flow of smoke-wreathed talk continued, with an occasional loud outburst and bang of knuckles on the table at a skillful play.

My companion and I were ignored, but I knew I was being checked out via Irish radar. Later there would be considerable talk and speculation about my companion and myself, which of course was why my friend had brought me to Maggie's in the first place.

Suddenly there was a strange, strangling sound at my side, and I glanced over just in time to see my erstwhile guide green-faced, hand to mouth, lurching hurriedly toward a door. The "secretary to the Taoiseach" was beating a mad retreat to the jacks, an ordinary citizen with the heaves from that one pint over the line. There was laughter in the air though I couldn't actually hear it, and I knew somehow that the attitude toward me was friendly.

WHITE'S
Between Dunmore East and Tramore
Take the shore road, and after a lovely, winding drive with glimpses of the sea you will arrive at a classic Irish whitewashed stone house with a thatched roof and a sign that says WHITE'S.

White's serves a local crowd. The day I visited was a Sunday, and the feeling in the big room was really neighborly and friendly. Whole families were there, from Grandma to baby, and I noticed a few good card games going.

It is a comfortable kind of place. At one end of the large room overstuffed chairs are arranged companionably around tables. At the other end a pool table and two dartboards are in constant use. White's is 150 years old and is owned by the genial and helpful John Doyle, a Dublin man who came here a few years ago and married a local girl.

Altogether befitting the pub's age and raftered charm are the many authentic rural artifacts that decorate it: stone jugs, stuffed grouse, a spinning wheel, a horse halter, animal skins, etc. My own favorite is a photo of three kittens and a hen. "She reared those kittens," John Doyle recalls, bemused. "She would cluck and they just used to get right up under her."

Of course, there's a big fireplace for a good blaze in winter. Wednesday and Saturday nights there is accordion and piano playing for a singsong.

KATEY REILLY'S KITCHEN
Midway on the Waterford–Tramore road

You are just coming from or are heading toward the lovely, sandy beaches of the area around Tramore. The road inland is straight and the countryside somewhat flat, so Katey Reilly's rises up like a real roadhouse. Although Katey's is a stop for tourists, it is enjoyed by the Irish as well and should not be missed.

It is said that the building was a farmhouse and shebeen when it was purchased in 1870 by the Power family. In 1890, with the advent of the licensing laws, Katey's, then called The Half-Way House, turned legal.

The structure of the old house itself has been retained, and there is a small parlor, a fireplaced main room, a cozy card room, and an attic dining room tucked away under the eaves. The whole is bursting from floor to ceiling with antiques collected over the years. A clutter of chairs, dolls, kettles, pots, farm implements, photographs, jugs and bugles, bedsteads and lamps, goats' heads, prams, antlers, swords, and bagpipes cover the walls and hang in profusion in every nook and cranny.

Among the amusing welter are some really unusual and valuable items, such as the two crested chairs given by Napoleon to James Napper-Tandy, a co-founder of the Society of United Irishmen, and the photo of "Pecker" Dunn, a famous traveling folk singer and traditional fiddler of the late nineteenth century. The owner and collector is Michael Brennan, and if you ask, either he or one of his witty assistants will point out to you the more interesting curios.

Attached to the old farmhouse is a renovated barn that is now a cabaret and dance hall featuring seven nights of music a week (four in winter). The music is generally rock and pop, except for the fortnightly evening of "trad."

The decor in the barn is pseudo-Tudor and rustic. A tree grows in the middle of the room, the tables are hand-hewn chunks of trees, the walls sport rare old whiskey and cigarette ads; old objects surface here and there, such as a graceful plow or a handmade harp. In the corner are two pool tables and a jukebox.

Food here is good: steak, curry, seafood, and delicious, homemade Irish brown bread.

THE SEANACHIE
Just outside Dungarvan on the Dungarvan–Cork road
Food: Excellent full menu

Winner of a "Top Pub" award, this is truly an exceptional public house: four stars, certainly, for The Seanachie.

The pub is a nest of three buildings forming a sheltered courtyard for pleasant outdoor drinking and dining. Its past varies with the historian; some say it was once the site of an abbey, others that it was a farm. Regardless, the proprietors have done a perfect job of restoration without the curse of "tweeness" (overquaintness).

Walls are a combination of whitewash and bare fieldstone; there is a walk-in fireplace giving forth the pungent odor of turf smoke and cooking soup. The soup is always aboil in a huge iron caldron slung over the fire as in the olden times. It tastes as good as it smells, utterly mouthwatering.

One building houses the bar, another a series of intimate dining nooks, the third a large hall for functions. The numerous fireplaces and the flowers on every table add to the atmosphere of bright welcome that is Ireland at its best.

COUNTY CORK

CORK

The Bells of Shandon

With deep affection,
And recollection,
I often think of
   Those Shandon bells,
Whose sounds so wild would,
In the days of childhood,
Fling around my cradle
   Their magic spells.
On this I ponder
Wher'er I wander,
   And thus grow fonder,
Sweet Cork, of thee;
With thy bells of Shandon,
That sound so grand on
   The pleasant waters of the River Lee.
      —Francis Sylvester Mahony
      (Father Prout)

There is the whole length of the quays, especially the pleasant bits where there are a few trees, such as the North Mall, or the Sand Quay, or the bit near the Opera House, though there only at particular hours, such as about five o'clock on a summer afternoon, or perhaps a little later than that, when the fishermen are drying or tarring their nets, and the angelus will soon be ringing in various tones and at various speeds all over the city, whose humming then slowly drops away into silence as the day ends. At such an hour Cork becomes without pretension the Lilliput it is. It offers no obstacle to the quiet tasting of quiet love. One season above all will haunt me, I know, and that for any corner of Cork—the time of the equinoctial gales: reminding us that Cork is a seaport and the sea at our door. Then the floods rise, the streets are sometimes submerged, and the winds of the ocean tear into the cup of the valley of the town. Then the age of the place, so well hidden under its rouge of paint (like a French seaport), is shamelessly exposed in the rattling and shaking and shivering and banging of all its poor decrepit parts. In these gales it flies in slivers through the air and, on mornings after gales, the streets where there are such houses are likely to be strewn with slates.

—Sean O'Faolain

The capital of Munster is the city of Cork, the Republic of Ireland's "second city," but to the Corkman there is not even a remote question of comparison with Dublin—"Rebel" Cork is quite simply superior.

Cork is called "rebel" because the rugged individualism of her natives embraces not only personality and style but also historical stance. Throughout the trials of centuries, the people of Cork staunchly remained true products of Erin, and conquering powers were soon assimilated, any allegiance to them being at best superficial.

The people of Cork have always shown a stubborn courage in the face of adversity. On three historic occasions they refused English rule: in the sixteenth century at the Reformation; at the end of the nineteenth century, during the Fenian Revolt; and at the beginning of the twentieth, with the "Troubles." The notorious IRA brigades of that era are held in especially high regard in Cork. Brendan Behan, in his *Brendan Behan's Island*, gives an eloquently humorous example of IRA commitment in Cork:

As I said, it's a very affluent city, Cork, with a good reputation for work, and it was there that Henry Ford in 1920 established their first European factory. Sometime thereabouts, the Cork Brigade of the I.R.A. were conducting some operations against the British that necessitated the use of motor transport—lorries—which the Brigade didn't have. Ford, of course, had plenty, so a few of the I.R.A. went down and held up the staff and the manager and demanded some lorries in the name of the Irish Republic.

The manager of the works, being a very clever and quick-thinking man, announced, "I'm sorry," said he, "you can't have any in the name of the Irish Republic because these works," he said, "are the property of a citizen of the United States of America with whom the Irish Republic is not at war."

But the commanding officer of the I.R.A. was what the times demanded of him, a quicker-thinking man, and he turned away and wrote something on a piece of paper. He turned back to the manager and, "Here," he said, "read that."

And the manager read out: "In the name of the Irish Republic, I solemnly do as from this moment declare war on the United States of America."

"Now," says the commanding officer, "hand over them bloody lorries quick."

The town of Cork is picturesquely situated clasped between the arms of the river Lee and clinging to the surrounding hilltops, yet in spite of its quaint quays and towers, the republic's highly important Atlantic seaport is a commercial nexus, the export center for the agricultural produce of the south.

There is a businesslike atmosphere about the main streets of Cork as the town hustles to press its new aggressive image as a rising modern center of industry and host to a gaggle of foreign manufacturers.

In spite of all this emphasis on trade, Cork maintains a proud tradition of support for the arts: ballet, theater, art, and music. The Cork Film Festival has somehow navigated through the rocky shoals of Irish censorship, and international stars and directors mingle in the pubs with the sportsmen and yachting enthusiasts, who are an ever-present phenomenon.

This tough, mercantile, yet poetic place has yielded a rich crop of writers: Sean O'Faolain, Frank O'Connor, and Daniel Corkery are all native sons whose work will reward the reader with special insight into the nature of life, universal, Irish, and Corkonian.

THE VINEYARD
Patrick Street

Owner Tom Kiernan is the third generation of Kiernans to run The Vineyard, and he's doing a fine job of it. The Vineyard is about 200 years old and has been renovated with great taste and style. It is a large, rambling pub with two snugs and the traditional partitions along the bar; the center of the room is capped with a superbly light, greenhouse-like, glass ceiling raised on a wooden base. This bit of inspired architecture lends an airy quality to the whole, which is fortunate, as the place is almost always dense with smoke and people.

The Vineyard caters to a mixed group of the young, the student, and the businessman. It is a particular favorite of the rugby crowd, both fans and players. After a few hours in The Vineyard you will soon understand why the city of Cork has such a reputation for being sports mad; much of the talk revolves around sports events, sports figures, sports stories, and even conversation itself is treated as a sport.

The people are exceptionally friendly and spontaneous, and I found myself invited to a dance down the road in a matter of moments. I couldn't go, having to keep a previous appointment. I took a taxi, and the driver said to me in his flat Cork accent, "Yiss, yiss, a nice girl like you requires a nice night life." It was raining; we drove along past dripping trees. An old man sat on a bench waiting for the bus. Behind him on the wall was written in black paint NO INTERNMENT.

TEACH BEAG
42 Oliver Plunkett Street
Tucked out of the way on Oliver Plunkett Street is this cozy little 150-year-old pub with old timber and brick walls, small tables, dim lights, a low ceiling, and a very crowded bar. It is run by Myra Halpin and her son Tom, who a few years ago redesigned the pub while adroitly maintaining its quality of intimate antiquity.

In this hangout of students from the nearby University College there is music and singing. The university is on the south side of the Lee, near the site, approximately, where St. Finbarr, established a monastery and school in the seventh century.

REARDEN'S CELLAR BAR
Washington Street
Rearden's is a newly reborn pub on an old site, a charming place for a delicious, inexpensive meal along with your pint. There are two good-sized rooms. The decor is stone and wood, with wooden barrels set into the walls. The long bar is made of shiny but not obtrusive pine supported on a base of kegs. The ceiling is beamed, and a pleasant atmosphere is created with rush baskets, old bottles, etc.

I sat in one of the roomy booths and enjoyed a well-cooked plaice, a fish I had not been acquainted with previously. "You've got a nice plaice here," I said to the waitress, unable to resist the pun. Quick as a flash the waitress parried with, "That's kind of a fishy compliment, isn't it?" In Cork no one minds the incorrigible punster.

THE OYSTER TAVERN
Market Lane (off Patrick Street)
Food specialty: Oysters, seafood

An elegant tavern is The Oyster Tavern, carpeted and polished, with old prints on the wall, cut glass, and heavy wooden chairs. Prior to 1828, one Widow Stokes held the premises under lease from Edward Barrett, a publican, and Richard Fitzgerald, a brewer.

There are a number of small dining salons, a fireplace, a main room, and a bar. The food is first-class, especially the seafood; and needless to say, oysters are triumphant here.

An additional note on the pubs of Cork: the game of darts is a highly esteemed form of recreation here, and you'll find a number of clubs and teams in heavy competition all over town.

THE TAIDY INN
Macroom—Cork road—about 15 minutes outside Cork
This tiny place is a 200-year-old coach house furnished with authentic antiques that made their way here from Belfast. There is a wee fire in the small lounge where you can sit at a wooden bench and table and enjoy excellent sandwiches or a cold platter.

YOUGHAL

Youghal is thirty miles from the city of Cork. It has several claims to fame besides its expansive beach: it is known for its point lace or "pointe d'Irlande," a lace with a vivid pattern; as well as Myrtle Grove, the stately Elizabethan building that was once Sir Walter Raleigh's home. According to tradition, Raleigh smoked the first tobacco to come to Ireland from the New World. As he sat puffing a pipe under a yew tree at Myrtle Grove, a servant, alarmed at the smoke, threw a bucket of water over his master to extinguish the fire. And it was in the garden at Myrtle Grove that Sir Walter is said to have grown the first spuds, plants brought from America.

MOBY DICK'S

The movie of Melville's epic novel was shot here in Youghal, and this pub commemorates it. There are three bars, a view of the harbor, and enough ship's wheels, hanging lanterns, and harpoons to satisfy the doughtiest tar.

The dartboard is popular, and a singsong starts evenings at 8:30.

AHERNE'S SEAFOOD BAR
North Main Street
Food specialty: Seafood
This jaunty, nautical pub is literally a prizewinner, having twice won Ireland's National Bar Food competition. The seafood *is* delicious and fresh.

KINSALE

Along the coast of County Cork is the inletted town of Kinsale, a popular summer resort for the Irish for two centuries. It has been adopted as well by the fashionable international set and the yachting crowd.

Kinsale has all the decayed charm of a seaport that technology has passed by. The town is terraced into the slope of Compass Hill with an almost Mediterranean charm, its narrow winding lanes bordered by a fine collection of crumbling Georgian houses. There are several cliff walks that are as wild and haunting as anything you can imagine. The stone circles of old Fort Charles afford a magical view of the town and a camper's paradise if you want to spend a night or two under the stars.

Kinsale is a meaningful place in Irish history: in 1601, the armies of the north under Hugh O'Neill (the Great O'Neill), Earl of Tyrone, suffered a decisive defeat here at the hands of the British Lord Deputy Mountjoy. Ever since, Kinsale has been synonymous with the final fighting failure of Gaelic society.

THE SPANIARD

High on Compass Hill, overlooking the sea, is a thatched and white-washed stone building with a sign depicting a dark and laughing cavalier—obviously the Spaniard in question. (The Irish have a special friendship with Spain dating back several centuries. A Spanish fleet fought alongside O'Neill in the battle against Mountjoy.)

Out front amid the flowers are a few tables and benches, excellent for watching the sunset and meeting convivial strangers. Within all is smoky-dim, low-ceilinged, and cozy. Built in the seventeenth century, the main room boasts a large fireplace and, for those who wish to watch more than the fire, a television set that can be turned on to reveal a mixture of news, BBC programs, *Kojak*, sports, and advertisements for farm implements. An adjoining room with small windows and ancient wooden tables is delightful for talk, drink, and cheese sandwiches. From a back room comes the sound of clicking billiard balls and laughter.

The clientele at The Spaniard is mainly Irish, of all ages, from a variety of counties, plus a smattering of international regulars. If you're so inclined, you can repair to the music room, where anyone can start a ballad and all join in for a singsong.

THE BULLMAN
Waterfront

Twilight at The Bullman is a special treat. The 200-year-old pub is situated directly on the quay, so you can wander out with your pint and watch the gulls turn iridescent in the sunset and listen to the gentle knocking of waves against stone.

Inside the small pub is a sweatered and rubber-booted bunch, most of whom know each other. You can't tell the fishermen from the yachtsmen here, and the American gone native is hard to tell from the Canadian who has settled here to earn his keep at fishing. There is a lot of good-natured ribbing about national quirks.

The foreigners in Kinsale are either old and rich or young and eccentric. The night I visited The Bullman, I met the younger crowd: two Australians, a Frenchman, a German, an Englishman, and an American. I also met an entire contingent of rather whimsical local people. It was a zany expatriate scene, and the American warned me not to stay over two days if I wanted to get away at all.

Main topics of conversation in Kinsale: boats, fishing, yachts, sailing, real estate (the Dutch and Germans have bought heavily in this area), and food. Kinsale has some of the best restaurants in all Ireland.

In October they celebrate a well-attended Gourmet Week.

Note: The founder of the State of Pennsylvania, William Penn, was clerk of the Admiralty Court in Kinsale.

The wreck of the *Lusitania* lies sunk off the coast. In 1914, the coroner at the inquest held in Kinsale brought in a verdict of murder against the Kaiser of Germany.

BANTRY

Encircled by gentle hills, Bantry dreams in the soft air. All manner of boats—spanking runabouts, Norwegian tunnies, royal yachts—bob at her quays. Bantry is a tourist center, but somehow the large square open to the sea breeze seems to be able to accommodate the buses without loss of tranquillity.

In 1979, the jolly blue of Bantry Bay was profaned by an oil spill. This abomination was cleaned up, but the specter of such pollution remains. Just off Whiddy Island in the bay is a Gulf Oil petroleum terminal where supertankers come to discharge their crude.

Not to be missed: Bantry House, built in 1750 and filled with a fine collection of tapestries and other works of art. Wander in the lush Italian gardens, the setting for the jewel that is the house; then repair to a pub.

THE ANCHOR INN

A typical pub of the area graced with, yes, an old anchor, along with fishermen's nets, photos, mounted fish, oil lamps, and so on. Pleasant.

BALLYDEHOB

Ballydehob

On the coast between Cork and Tralee,
and quite easy adjacent the sea,
Far away from the maddening mob
Lies mellifluous Ballydehob.

Skibereen, to the east, sounds, I think,
Like a marble dropped into a sink;

It has none of the glorious throb
of melodious Ballydehob.

Just off to the west there lies Schull,
'Tis a name over which you could mull
But you can't roll it 'round in your gob
Like euphonious Ballydehob.

'Tis a picturesque sort of a place,
Full of Irish, a charmin' old race;
Just stravage into Ballydehob
And bejabbers! your uncle is Bob!

Was there ever a village could claim
A more dulcet, harmonious name?
Sure, the fella he did a great job
When he said, "Call it Ballydehob!"
—William Rossa Cole
(Grandson of Donovan Rossa)

This little West Cork community is a thriving artists' and writers' colony of some renown and a haven for artistic international dropouts (some famous) from all over the world. The shops and houses are painted different refreshing pastel colors. The stores contain some beautiful local crafts for you to bring home: batik, candles, pottery, paintings, sculpture, and hand-woven rugs. This is not the usual tourist mass-produced junk but art created by true artisans.

GABE'S PLACE
Gabe and Michelle Hannon run a place where the pints are fit for a king and "the crack" is good. The neat, stone-floored, 120-year-old pub was artfully redone by Gabe, using beams from the London Stock Exchange for the ceiling. (Does that make Gabe's a good place for speculation, I wonder.) The walls are stone, there is a cozy snug, and if you look around, you will notice some fine pewter collected by Gabe.

The original building itself was a 220-year-old mill, and the wheel is still there. At a side entrance and upstairs Gabe operates a good restaurant, The Old Mill.

SCHULL

A few miles from Ballydehob is Schull, another artists' center and favorite port of call for international yachtsmen.

Schull is a small fishing village sheltered from the north winds by
Mt. Gabriel. From the harbor you can see the group of islands known as
the Carbery's Hundred Islands. Take the ferry for an afternoon on Cape
Clear Island, a wind-swept, green-carpeted, flower-strewn rock where
life is old and custom timeless. On the way you will see the solitary
Fastnet Rock lighthouse, Ireland's most southern point.

Schull is basically a fishing port, five trawlers and about ten smaller
fishing boats fish out of the perfect little harbor. There is a fish-
processing plant at the pier, and a supply of fresh fish is readily available: crab, lobster, crayfish, prawns, salmon, mackerel, scallops, and
all types of whitefish.

TOM NEWMAN'S—CORNER HOUSE
Main Street

Tom Newman's *is* on the corner. It is a grocery shop–pub and a center
for local news, as well as a good spot for a spontaneous musical inter-
lude. Newman's is a racing sailors' and fishermen's pub, and it is here
that you apply for your permit to fish the reservoir for the rainbow trout
stocked there. The talk is equally divided between fish and regattas,
both of which abound here in West Cork.

This pub is always lively, but it is particularly amusing during Schull
Festival Week (usually sometime in mid-July). My favorite event of the
festival, aside from the singing competition, is the pub-to-pub wheel-
barrow race.

THE BLACK SHEEP INN
Main Street

This is a truly quaint, rambling old inn with a charming entrance
through an alleyway and a back garden. The pub features both spontaneous and organized music and is furnished comfortably.

Seafood, salads, and steaks are to be had upstairs.

Overheard at The Black Sheep Inn: "There's a lot of truth to the lies
you tell."

SOME NOTES ON THE WEST CORK AREA

In this area Ireland outdoes herself in treats for the visitor: you can easily rent boats, go deep-sea fishing or diving (see the harbor master in Schull), go pony trekking (Schull or Bantry), rent bikes (Schull), play tennis (courts outside Schull) or golf (Bantry or Skibbereen).

Day trips and walks could keep you in the area for weeks. Glengariff, while pretty much overrun with tourists, is a must. A little village on the Beara peninsula, it snuggles in a mythically fertile glen. The valley, though rocky, is thickly wooded with oaks, elms, pines, yew, and holly, as well as various Mediterranean-type plants flowering their hearts out. Visit Garinish Island there and the exceptional gardens open to the public. Glengariff will make a poet out of you. Even if you can't write it down, the ancient spell woven of water, air, light, and foliage will never be forgotten.

If you are driving on a Sunday in West Cork, be careful. Just around the next bend you might encounter a favorite pastime, road bowling. A 28-ounce cast-iron ball is lofted across a curve and flung along a measured course on the road, drawing an excited Sunday crowd of betters.

CASTLETOWNBERE

All around are the wild greys and greens of West Cork; the hundred islands of Roaringwater Bay in a flecked sea that for weeks has been unaccountably blue. Under this crazy sunshine it is like an unnaturally fertilised Greece. It is, probably, so far, the last "unspoiled" place on the seashores of Europe—it won't last long; already the harbingers from England and Germany are moving in with their infiltrating property deals; the locals are beginning to learn the value of a bit of a field with a view, and the strangers abound. You can identify visitors by the fact that they alone wear native jerseys and Irish homespun.

For some reason it seems more sympathetic than anywhere else.

—James Cameron

The peninsulas of southwest Ireland reach into the sea like the paw of a bear reaching for a fish. Oddly, one of the wildest and most romantic of these peninsulas is called Beara. At the tip of this jumble of misty mountain–forest lies the town of Castletownbere.

It was in driving to this sleepy fishing village that I received a lesson in Irish time. At the top of one of the mountain passes beside a rocky waterfall, my car, after a few dispiriting thumpety-thumps, limped to a halt, sighed, settled, and let all the air out of the punctured left front tire. I hitchhiked to the nearest garage, sitting curled around my tire in the back seat of a Renault, a feat worthy of the Incredible Rubber Man.

The garageman's verdict was that the tire would be ready in half an hour. An hour later I inquired. He suggested a nice place down the road for a "cupa tay" or a pint. Another half an hour and I began to frown, in spite of the lovely landscape I found myself in. After more delay, I became what used to be described as wroth.

The man eyed me with a calm twinkle. "Sure, and what'll the world be without ye when yer gone?" he said. I deflated in a fine imitation of my tire. In Ireland no one hurries and time is truly relative; it is the broth in which events are savored.

O'DONAGHUE'S BAR
Main Square
Wide and sun-drenched, Main Square is bordered at one end by a pier and at the other sides by higgledy-piggledy pastel houses.

O'Donaghue's is an unprepossessing, typical, dark old pub; but the feeling is friendly, and you can't beat the location.

Among the fishermen who live and work in Castletownbere are many transplanted Dutch and English people. Tourism, however, is not that apparent here, and in O'Donaghue's you'll find mainly locals and the odd, sturdily booted student with his faithful knapsack.

Have a pint and then go to view the ruins of Dunboy Castle.

Dunboy Castle stands on a promontory with the Atlantic spreading before it. At one time it belonged to a powerful Irish prince, O'Sullivan Beare.

An ally of the Great O'Neill, he, too, went down to gallant defeat in the battle of Kinsale, the struggle that marked the end of Celtic-Norman Ireland. In the aftermath, Dunboy Castle was ravaged and many of his people massacred.

In a story that is the ultimate Irish tale of romantic heroism, O'Sullivan refused to surrender and fought his way north with his people, against impossible odds. Here is the edict circulated by the Lord President in 1602, calling on everyone "on peril of being treated as O'Sullivan's covert or open abettors, to fall upon him, to cross his road, to bar his way, to watch for him at fords, to come upon him by night; and, above all, to drive off or destroy all cattle or other possible means of sustenance, so that of sheer necessity his party must perish on the way. Whose lands soever O'Sullivan would be found to have passed through unresisted, or whereupon he was allowed to find food of any kind, the Government would consider forfeit."

In 1603 Lord Deputy Mountjoy wrote to the Privy Council: "All that are out do seek for mercy excepting O'Rorke and O'Sullivan, who is now with O'Rorke." Of the thousand souls who started on the journey with O'Sullivan, only about a hundred made it to O'Rorke's castle in Leitrim. In 1604, O'Sullivan, despairing of effective resistance, left Ireland for exile in Spain, where he was murdered coming home from Mass.

Next to the stump of Dunboy Castle is the fire-gutted ruin of Puxley Hall, looking like the cover of a gothic paperback romance. It was built in 1920 by a wealthy Welsh landowner. The fire that razed it to the ground was the work of Irish rebels, but if you ask about it, you'll be deflected with pleasant Irish vagaries—even now.

CASTLETOWNSHEND

Castletownshend is a particularly pretty Irish village with a steeply inclined street that, charmingly enough, sports an oak tree right in the middle. The large oak serves two purposes: it is a delight, and it acts as a leafy barrier to buses bearing hordes of tourists.

MARY ANN'S BAR

Mary Ann's claims to be the oldest pub in Ireland. The tiny, dark bar with a low ceiling and beat-up old table is just the place to be on a rainy day; at sunny times lunch and drinks are served in a back garden under a shady grape arbor. Dinner is served upstairs in the pub, in a cozy alcove.

The clientele is a mixture of locals and low-key summer people. There is a large billiard table, and a dartboard in one of the rooms, which is popular with the locals. When the occasion warrants, the billiard table gives way to a dance floor for local hops.

Food: there is usually a choice of lobster, salmon, or one other main course, as well as soup and pâté. Salads are also available.

COUNTY KERRY

For many people, Kerry is like the geographical crock of gold at the end of Ireland's rainbow, for it boasts the three large and jagged peninsulas of Beara, Iveragh, and Dingle—those misty regions of ancient Celtic magic.

The most traveled of the three, Iveragh, takes you on the first leg of the famous "Ring of Kerry," a stretch of road that offers rare and awe-inspiring vistas. At the base of Iveragh lies that hive of tourist activity, Killarney.

KILLARNEY

The town itself is a traffic jam in the summer, and its natives are well versed in dispensing professional Irish charm. It is an expensive place geared to the busloads of tourists that are disgorged in front of the Great Southern Hotel.

The vale of Killarney, however, in which the town nestles, is so beautiful that Brendan Behan once said, ". . . even an ad man would be ashamed to eulogize it."

Three main lakes occupy a broad valley stretching south between the mountains. These lakes are surrounded by luxuriant woods of oak, arbutus, birch, holly, and mountain ash. The ground is soft with moss and the air fragrant with flowery freshness. Cars are barred from the many ferny trails, so take a rewarding hike or hire a "jarvey," a horse and old-fashioned jaunting car, left over from the days when the Victorians discovered Killarney and painted and poeticized it into world popularity.

Like as not, the jarvey driver will be giving out plenty of blarney for tourist consumption (a favorite trick: "Ah, and there's one of the wee folk right over there under that bush—ah, ya just missed him"), but take him in along with the scenery.

KATE KEARNEY'S
Gap of Dunloe
(About 5 miles outside Killarney)

Here you can take refreshment at the same cottage where once the elegantly attired Victorians sipped illegal "poteen" (potato spirits a little like Tennessee's White Lightning) prepared for them by Kate herself. Then, fortified, you will be ready for the Ice Age miracles of the Gap of Dunloe. All cars are left behind and you descend into this cleft in the earth on foot or by pony trap.

Transferring to a boat, you are then treated to a romantic's fantasy come true as you slide along the lakes, great boulders to either side. You pass places with names like "The Devil's Punchbowl" and "The Eagles' Nest," said to be the last refuge of the Irish eagle.

There are a number of other sights in this area, but a real *must* is Muckross. A nineteenth-century manor house on the middle lake, set in subtropical gardens, the trails lead you through masses of rhododendrons and azaleas, as well as water, woodland, and rock gardens.

After these pleasures, perhaps you can brave the town for a jar or a pint.

CAHERDANIEL

Caherdaniel is a peaceful retreat on the famous Ring of Kerry route, which brings you around the entire coast of Iveragh. It is situated near the shore of Derrynane Bay, where hillsides patterned with fields "the forty shades of green" slip gently to the water's edge. (Just as the Eskimos, surrounded by snow, have many words for different varieties, so the Irish say that there are forty shades of green in their Emerald Isle. I believe them.)

Nearby is the haunting hermitage of St. Crohane, hewn entirely from solid rock, as well as an ancient stone fort, every stone put into position without benefit of mortar of any kind.

Also in the vicinity is Derrynane House, the restored home of Daniel O'Connell, "the Liberator."

In the early nineteenth century the situation for Catholics in Ireland was intolerable—they had no rights whatsoever. Daniel O'Connell, an eloquent Catholic lawyer from Kerry, roused the people, organizing them in "monster rallies" of protest demanding Catholic emancipation and the repeal of the Act of Union, which had joined Ireland and England.

While he did not gain independence from England, he was successful in emancipating Irish Catholics and in helping to restore their pride. O'Connell was important not only to the Ireland of his own time; he was the father of today's use of nonviolent mass action. Like Martin Luther King, Jr., he rallied and embodied the spirit and will of his people.

FREDDY'S
Whether it be a pound of spuds or a bit of crack you're after, Freddy's will cater to you. In the front is a shop carrying practically everything and in the rear, through swinging doors, a bar and tables for a pint of porter.

If you grab a seat in the corner early on a Sunday morning, you are likely to overhear conversations ranging from sheep prices on the Beara peninsula to the latest anti-nuke demonstrations.

The ceilings are very low, giving the place a cozy feel. Freddy presides over the solid oak bar, opening the back door sometimes to let the flow of smoke out.

The toilets are located at the other side of an open courtyard, giving one a tan or pneumonia, depending on the weather.

The only bar in town, Freddy's gets them all.

CAHIRCIVEEN

The ends of peninsulas always seem to produce a feeling of loneliness and wind-washed clarity that nourishes the brain and stimulates the sense of wonder. Technology and politics don't make it out to the ends of the earth, and the people live in simple ways that reflect this welcome absence.

Cahirciveen is one such town, situated far out on the Iveragh peninsula at the foot of Bantee Mountain, overlooking the sea and Valentia
Island (particularly popular with deep-sea anglers). In the summer, a
number of artists and art students come here to paint, drawn by the
beauty and the presence of an art school.

MAGUIRE'S

Paddy and Pauline Maguire have run this tiny place for many years and
are known to discerning people all over Ireland. I first heard about Maguire's from the Irish writer and raconteur Ben Kiely, who listed it as a
particular favorite.

The stores and houses that line the main street of an Irish town seem
to have grown there, so naturally do they bend and blend with their
surroundings, forming a unity with street, hills, and sky. In one of these
houses that makes up the main street of Cahirciveen is Maguire's, a
tiny, cluttered shop/bar. The day I arrived, Pauline, a small, salt-and-
peppery woman, served me over the worn counter-bar in the dark little
front room. She chatted easily, her sharp eyes taking me in all the
while. From a curtained door came the sounds of television. "Come
in," she said, inviting me through the curtain.

Several elderly men with pints by their sides were sitting in a living
room watching the TV with rapt attention. The International Equestri-
an Jumping Competition was being televised from Germany. Ireland's
entry, Eddie Macken, had been a previous champion on a horse named
Kerry Gold, and the talk was about his chances of winning again.

Horses are very dear to the Irish, and everyone in the room was im-
mersed in the elegant images of formal perfection, of unity between
horse and rider, that were reaching into the little back room all the way
from Germany.

I looked around. It is somehow extraordinary to find yourself doing
your official drinking in the living room of a perfect stranger—even in
Ireland. It's not unusual to an Irishman, though. The custom dates
back to the days of illegal poteen, and though growing fewer by the
year, places like Maguire's can still be found in the countryside.

The room was furnished with comfortable, faded old chairs and a
nice old sofa. There were several tables with oilcloth coverings, pic-

tures of children in First Communion dress, people in wedding clothes, and an amazing number of odd items hanging from the ceiling, such as woven baskets from Trinidad, mounted fish, dolls, etc.

Pauline refreshed my drink, and we watched the contest in a silence interspersed with small bursts of congenial talk. The silvery sunlight of the late Irish afternoon moved across the room, and I wished I could stay forever. It was like visiting a favorite aunt.

THE EVANS HOTEL
Specialty: Sole Walenski
The Evans Hotel was built in 1893 as an elegant private residence. The paintings, furnishings, and architecture have not been tampered with, which gives the place the tranquil flavor of days gone by.

The bar is in the back, and either Mary Jo or her husband, Tom Evans, will be happy to pull you a pint. Mary Jo will even top off your Guinness with a foam shamrock. Mrs. Evans is an impressive person altogether. She's a dark-haired beauty, elegantly turned out and very articulate, a painter in winter when business is slack. "Ah, it's a poor fish that never has a Guinness," she said pertly in answer to my praise of that national resource.

Her husband, Tom, is equally diverting and an excellent chef. His specialty (delicious) is sole in sauce Walenski.

Looking around in the snug little bar with the draped windows, I saw numerous old prints and etchings decorating the walls: the launching of the *Titanic*, the romantic castle of Macroom. The crenellated entrance, the gate, and part of the old walls of this fairy-tale castle still dominate the town square of Macroom.

William Penn, who was born at Macroom Castle and lived there till the age of three, would have been astounded at the use his birthplace is put to today: in the summer, the fields behind the gate, where once the castle stood, are the site of outdoor rock festivals; hundreds of young fans converge on the grassy hillsides to relax, drink beer, and listen to their favorite bands.

After properly Irish musings on the vagaries of time embodied in the etching of Macroom, I rose to go. The old-fashioned phone behind the bar started to ring raucously. "I better answer that phone before it hops

off its handle," said Mary Jo. I smiled and went to the dining room to
find out what Walenski knew about sole sauces and what Tom knew
about Walenski.

GLENBEIGH

Just outside Cahirciveen, between the road and the sea, is the peak of
Knocknadober Mountain. On this peak in pagan days Lughnassa, the
harvest festival, was celebrated. There is a well on the mountain that in
later Christian times was dedicated to Fursa, an Irish saint presiding
over visions.

To be sure, the road from Cahirciveen northeast to Glenbeigh is as
beautiful as any vision you could wish for from St. Fursa. Literally one
of the high points of the Ring of Kerry, the road skirts the heights over
Dingle Bay, affording majestic views across to the mist-shrouded peaks
of Dingle Peninsula. The road gradually descends to the little town of
Glenbeigh, beloved of many nationalities but not overrun or overcom-
mercialized.

Glenbeigh is situated at the entrance to a horseshoe of mountains
where the Bethy River flows into Dingle Bay. Take one of the numerous mountain walks, or if you're lazy, go on horseback, or cross the
stone bridge and picnic along the ferny banks of the river. The bridge,
by the way, like most Irish bridges, is the type preferred by trolls.

About two miles from Glenbeigh is Rossbeigh beach, one of the
loveliest in all Ireland. Miles of sandy beach backed by dunes stretch
along the bay. The rounded, female curves of ancient mountains rise in
the distance (no wonder "Mother Ireland"), and nearby is the protective presence of Curra Hill, purple with heather in the spring.

From Glenbeigh, it is three miles, via the Windy Gap, Blackstones
Bridge, and the course of the Caragh River to Glencar, a climbing and
angling center in a wild valley full of pure, rushing water, flowers, and
cloud shadow.

EVANS TOWERS
Food: European cuisine   *Specialty:* Salmon mousse
Evans Towers is a landmark in Kerry. Its proprietor, Ernie Evans, a

large, affable man with a faint resemblance to Sydney Greenstreet, is famous as a raconteur, chef, and behind-the-scenes politician (I got the impression that his fame made him a somewhat controversial figure).

The pub occupies the ground floor of a century-old house and is filled every night with a disparate crowd of merrymakers: locals from the farmworker to the landowner, vacationing Irish professional people, fishermen, students, tourists, and assorted characters.

The large front room, low-ceilinged for warmth, has a bar and live music and singing. The adjoining rooms are small and cozy, buzzing with talk and laughter.

On warm nights, the crowd spills outside onto a kind of stone apron to hold forth to one another, pints in hand.

The food is quite good. There is a large variety of dishes; but the starters are better than quite good—they are outstanding. Try the delicious creamy salmon mousse.

KILLORGLIN

Normally a quiet little town composed mainly of pubs (52), Killorglin becomes a focal point for thousands of people once a year, in August. The occasion is Puck Fair, one of the last vestiges of pagan fertility rites in Europe. There's a legend that "Puck" commemorates an occasion when the stampeding of goats gave warning of the approach of English forces.

Puck Fair is a horse-and-cattle fair, a musical event, an orgiastic release celebrating life-energy, full of brawling, drinking, and wheeler-dealering. While the event *has* been much commercialized, its spirit somehow survives. Be forewarned, however, of all the inconveniences of a small area inundated by a large crowd.

While Puck Fair belongs to everyone, it is of particular importance to the tinkers or "traveling people," for it is their annual gathering of the clan, and they congregate here from all parts of Ireland. These people have wandered over Ireland in horse-drawn caravans for centuries. Their origin is unclear, but it is probable that they became itinerants as a result of all the land evictions, the Cromwell exile west, and the penal times (see page 195).

Theirs is a hard life; they have survived by tinsmithing, horse-trading, building poteen stills, and begging. Many superstitions surround this close-knit, tribal society of indigenous gypsies; they are thought to possess special magic powers.

Like many itinerant or minority societies, they have had to develop their own secret language, *cant gamin*, which they use when they want to conceal what they say to one another from outsiders.

An aside: When around tinker children, you'd be well advised to watch your pockets and purse. They are extraordinarily quick, both with wit and with fingers. I once saw a crowd of children no older than five or six surround a woman; while they distracted her with begging, one of them calmly helped himself to the contents of her pockets. From the tinker viewpoint there is no question of ethics here. The children are taught to pick pockets as part of the business of survival.

So strong is the clan tradition and structure that descendants of the traveling people who emigrated to the United States over one hundred years ago still carry on their nomadic life there, some ten thousand or so, ranging from the Atlantic coast of Georgia to as far west as Oklahoma.

> The daily language of the tinkers is the countryman's English of perhaps a hundred years ago. Up till now, their journeyings had insulated them against the standardized English taught in the National Schools; they could hardly know that talk is supposed to be pale and wan. Literacy, which can paralyze speech with propriety, was never needed in their lives. On the road, it would not refine the making of tinware, nor would it pitch a wattle tent or help put the canvas over that tent's hooped branches. But now, for the first time in the history of their world, to read and write is to enter life; the old ones have chosen settlement on account of their children, who they rightly perceive would be at a greater disadvantage without education than they themselves could ever be. At the end of the road, there is no place to go but the schoolhouse.
>
> —Lawrence Millman

Another aside. The Bothy Band, one of Ireland's best traditional bands, was founded by tinkers.

Joining the tinkers, the farmers, the cattle, the pigs, the horses, and the tourists that swarm through the narrow, Old World streets are itinerant balladeers and fiddlers from all over Ireland, passing the hat at every corner. For three days the bars stay open twenty-four hours, given over to total bacchanalia.

Reigning over all is the King of the Fair, the Puck, a fine male goat ensconced on a platform above the heads of the swirling crowd.

By late afternoon of "Gathering Day"—normally August 10—the crowds are sparking with anticipation. The men of the town have returned from Macgillycuddy's Reeks, the magnificent range to the south, one of whose peaks, Carrantuohill (the Left-Handed Reaping Hook), is the highest in Ireland. They have brought back unharmed the largest and handsomest he-goat they could find.

Accompanied by the enthusiastic crowd and a band of pipes, drums, and flutes, the Puck is taken to the town square and crowned by a young girl (the obligatory virgin). Decorated and beribboned, he is then raised by a pulley system to the top of a three-tiered 52-foot platform (hung with an enormous banner advertising Guinness), from which he will reign for the next three days.

When Puck reaches the top, the excited crowd bursts into dancing, which will continue for the next three nights. At sunset of the third day (Scattering Day), the Puck is dethroned and set free, but the reveling continues till dawn.

While all this tradition is very romantic, the reality of the festival is commercial, simple, loud, earthy, humorous, inconvenient, and brawling. A fine coat of dung covers the streets and drunkenness abounds. Any attempt to dwell on its symbolic significance is met with instant ridicule, for only by denying the strictures of official ritualization can a festival like this remain alive—and alive it most certainly is.

THE OLD FORGE

Out of the mass of bars in Killorglin, The Old Forge is one of the most authentic, from the thatched roof to the used fishing net on the ceiling. It has a good-size bar, the ever-present lounge, and—surprise—a courtyard with two saunas.

Naturally, The Old Forge should receive your patronage, especially during Puck Fair, when a sauna is just the thing you need to keep you going.

DINGLE PENINSULA

O Gaelic, most sweet and soft of sound,
Swift, robust, as the waves of the sea,
Trodden and trampled, despised by all—
That you live at all is a wonder to me!
                                        —Peader O'Doirnin

Dingle Peninsula stretches thirty spectacular miles into the Atlantic. Like Beara it is wild and mystical, but Dingle is more barren and possesses a greater sense of timeless prehistory. Here language is old, too— this is the Gaeltacht, the area where Gaelic is still spoken and taught.

Great cliffs fall hundreds of feet to the sea, vistas of light-blessed grandeur unfold before you as you travel the narrow coast roads. One can wander with J. M. Synge:

I walked up this morning along the slope from the east to the top of Sybil Head, where one comes out suddenly on the brow of a cliff with a straight fall of many hundreds of feet into the sea. It is a place of indescribable grandeur, where one can see Carrantuohill and the Skelligs and Loop Head and the full sweep of the Atlantic, and over all, the wonderfully tender and searching light that is seen only in Kerry. Looking down the drop of five or six hundred feet, the height is so great that the gannets flying close over the sea look like white butterflies, and the choughs like flies fluttering behind them. One wonders in these places why anyone is left in Dublin, or London, or Paris, when it would be better, one would think, to live in a tent or hut with this magnificent sea and sky, and to breathe this wonderful air, which is like wine in one's teeth.

Monks were attracted to this special place to live and pray, not in tents, but in stone clochans, beehive-shaped shelters that speak to us movingly of a simple faith still grounded in nature.

Stone forts and crosses abound, and myths hang in the air on the verge of becoming visible. Standing on the beach at Ventry, you can easily picture the events said to have taken place there. Daire Doon, the primeval King of the World, arriving in his colorful ships to conquer Ireland and meeting defeat on the beach at the hands of the giant Finn MacCool and his warriors, the Fianna.

Modern fables, too, have taken place on Dingle: *Ryan's Daughter* was filmed here, and an entire Irish village, Kirrary, built for it. After the film, the town was dismantled, but the experience lingers in the conversation of the Dingle natives.

The mother goddess has always had a strong hold on the Kerry imagination, coming to them in many mystic guises: the Hag of Beara, the Sky Woman, and here in Dingle, the Fair Lady Banba, who dwells in the mountains of Slieve Mish. It is said that her influence generates a wild restlessness in these hills. So if it's primal nature and Celtic romance you're after, make your headquarters in Dingle and explore the peninsula.

> Oftentimes now there were gentlemen to be seen about the roads, some young and others aged, addressing the poor Gaels in awkward unintelligible Gaelic and delaying them on their way to the field. The gentlemen had fluent English from birth but they never practised this noble tongue in the presence of Gaels lest, it seemed, the Gaels might pick up an odd word of it as a protection against the difficulties of life. . . . They rambled about the countryside with little black notebooks for a long time before the people noticed that they were not *peelers* but gentlefolk endeavouring to learn the Gaelic of our ancestors and ancients. As each year went by, these folk became more numerous. Before long the place was dotted with them. With the passage of time, the advent of spring was no longer judged by the flight of the first swallow but by the first Gaeligore seen on the roads. They brought happiness and money and high revelry with them when they came; pleasant and funny were these creatures, God bless them.
>
> —Myles na Gopaleen (Flann O'Brien)

DINGLE

O'FLAHERTY'S

Dingle is a small fishing and local merchants' town (pop. 1,000) on the sea surrounded on three sides by hills. Across from the police station, beside the sea, is O'Flaherty's, one large barnlike room with a long bar on one side and a raised platform for musicians on another. There's a fine musician named Ferguson who plays here. He's a master of the tin whistle, accordion, banjo, and probably some others I haven't heard of.

If you want a bodhran (Irish goatskin drum) specially made and hand-painted for you, this is the place to ask about it.

The pub is around 150 years old, with red-timbered walls and the bar-counter high enough that, as a regular confided to me, "when ya put yer elbows down, the drink rushes to yer head faster." Photographs, old advertisements, and poetry are pinned up on rough walls, and it's enjoyable to wander around, pint in hand, reading.

You'll always find a hearty welcome at O'Flaherty's, especially in August at the time of the annual Curragh races, when the talk is either about the day's race or the oyster catch. The crowd is made up of Dingle fishermen and local people, students of the Gaelic language, tourists, and a variety of elegant folk "roughing it"—writers, intellectuals, politicians, and businessmen all fleeing the rigors of their lives. Many have remote houses to which they retire, coming out in the evening to gather in the conviviality generated at O'Flaherty's.

I was introduced to this warmhearted pub by a Swedish woman who had come to Dingle to study Gaelic with Sean Murphy of Ballinskelligs. Sean is a farmer and a shanachie. A shanachie is a storyteller—the weaver of word magic—the man who holds the long oral tradition of Irish lore in his head. Unfortunately, shanachies are a disappearing breed.

Sean teaches his class in Gaelic, saying whatever comes into his head; talking of the Kerry poets Tomas Roe O'Sullivan and Owen Roe O'Sullivan, or of the old customs and community life as it was lived.

Owen Roe O'Sullivan is a Kerry hero of sorts. He was a peasant-poet of the 1700s, an itinerant potatodigger and devastating ladies' man. There are as many stories of his amazing bawdy powers as there are versions of his poetry.

Owen Roe is the last of a Kerry tradition of wandering poets; but you can still hear poetry in the everyday speech of the Kerry people, and Kerry-born Brendan Kennelly is a world-renowned poet of today.

Saturday, the 16th of September, 1769, will be sold or set up for sale, at Skibbereen, the robust horse Spanker, the property of Thomas O'Donnell, Esq. A strong, staunch, steady, sound, stout, sinewy, safe, serviceable, strapping, supple, swift, smart, sightly, sprightly, spirited, shining, sure-footed, sleek, smooth, spunky, well-skinned, -sized and -shaped: a sorrel steed of superlative symmetry, styled Spanker, and a snip square-sided, slender-shouldered, smart-sighted, with a small star, and steps singularly stately; free from strain, sprain, spasm, stringhalt, stranguary, sciatica, staggers, sealing, sollander, surfeit, seams, scouring, strangle, strenuous swelling, soreness, scratches, splint, squint, squirt, scruff, scales, scurp, scars, scabs, scarred sores, scattering, shuffling, shambling gait or symptoms of sickness of any sort. He is neither stiff-mouthed, shabby-coated, sinew-shrunk, spur-galled, nor saddle-backed, shell-toothed, slim-gutted, sunbated, skin-scabbed, short-winded, splay-footed or shoulder-slipped, and is sound in the sword-point and stiffle-joint, has neither sick spleen, sleeping-evil, set-fast, or snaggle-tooth, nor suppression of urine, sand-creaks, swelling-sheath, subcutaneous sores, or shattered hoofs, is not sour, sulky, slow, surly, stubborn, or sullen in temper, neither shy, sly, nor skittish, slow, sluggish, nor stupid. He never slips, slides, strays, stalks, stops, starts, shakes, swells, snivels, snibbles, snuffles, smarts, stumbles, or stocks in his stall or stable, and scarcely or seldom sweats, has a showy, skittish switch tail or stern, and a safe set of shoes to stride on. He can feed on stubbles, sheaf-outs, straw, sedges and scotch grass, carries 16 stones on his stroke with surprising speed over a six-foot sod or stone wall. His sire was the sly, sober Sydus on a sister of Spindle Shanks by Sampson and Sporter, son of Sparkler who won the Sweepstake and Subscription Plate last season at Sligo. His selling price is sixty-six pounds, sixteen shillings and sixpence sterling. [from an exercise in English by

Owen Roe O'Sullivan]

The Black Cliffs, Ballybunion

White horses galloping on the sand
Toss their beautiful Atlantic manes
At girls selling seagrass and
Periwinkles. Whatever pain
Is in God's heart is in the sea
That batters the black cliffs where I stand,
Aware of love's infinity
And how infinitely little I understand.
A man is carting seaweed near the rocks
Where I saw a brother and sister drown
Only three summers ago;

A curlew cries where the sea breaks, gathers, breaks;
God cries passionately to be known
But who would dare to begin to know?
                                                        —Brendan Kennelly

DUNQUIN

KRUGER'S PUB

Off Slea Head at the tip of Dingle Peninsula lie the Blasket Islands.
Beyond, according to Celtic fable, is Tir-na-nog, land of perpetual
youth, the Beyond Otherworld. Actually, what lay beyond the Blaskets
was another world—America. The Blasket Islands are the most western
lands in Europe.

In 1953, life on these windswept stones became untenable for the
few who still clung to them, and the last inhabitants were moved to the
mainland. Many settled in Dunquin.

You'll probably find some of these islanders in Kruger's, a fine place
for the dance and the singsong and, if you're lucky, the memory or tale
well told. Or perhaps you'll get a genuine Irish viewpoint on those who
played at being Irish—the crew and cast of *Ryan's Daughter* used to
come to Kruger's for rest and rehabilitation.

The currach, the prehistoric boat built and used by Dingle fishermen
for centuries, still plays an important role here in Dingle. These canoes
are made of tarred canvas stretched over an open lattice framework.
They are about eighteen feet long, and there are usually four rowers,
each pulling two almost bladeless oars. Three passengers, all sitting in
the bottom of the boat, make a full load. Ask at Kruger's about renting
one to take you on a trip to Great Blasket. Before you set out, read a bit
of Maurice O'Sullivan's *Twenty Years A-Growing*, Peig Sayer's *Peig*, or
Letters from the Great Blasket by Eibhlis Ni Shúilleabháin. For a telling
contemporary viewpoint not only on the Gaeltacht but on how the
Irish view themselves, read David Hanly's *In Guilt and in Glory*.

8/21/33: They are in from the sea here with the last few days, I mean the
fishermen. The sea is rough and wild, so they have another job cutting

the corn, also bringing home the turf. The fishermen have a small bottle
of holy-water in every canoe, and I often saw them when going into the
canoe, for to go fishing of course, would make the sign of the Cross. I am
sure they have no certain prayers for it only to ask the Lord to bring them
back home safe.

9/11/37: I think Mr. Synge was the first visitor that ever visited Blaskets.
That time of course they were not as well and able and smart like they are
in the lodging houses today.

11/10/38: I am always on the look out for what Synge wrote about Blasket
and I suppose I would not ever read it only for you, thanks ever so much.
As far as I understand it I think he wrote excelantly [sic] about Blasket.
He wrote more to the credit of the place than what he had seen as far as I
remember my own childhood days . . . and there is an awful change on
Blasket since Synge was here. I would call Synge a clean and splendid
writer for Blasket anyway. All the Blasket people anyhow thought Synge
wrote awkwardly about this place and now they do not think so. So to
conclude . . . I should say for the Final that he was a clean and decent
writer.

Eibhlis Ni Shúilleabháin
—*Letters from the Great Blasket*
(written to George Chambers of London
after he visited Great Blasket in 1931)

Halsam said with a grimace of disgust, "Here we are in the heart of the
Gaeltacht. Probably every boy and girl of them born and reared to glorious natural Gaelic, and now listen to them spewing out that dreadful goo
that they pick up every night on TV. If the British had had TV in the
seventeenth century they wouldn't have had to send a single soldier to
Ireland." He looked down in disgust at the scene below them.

"They can't shed their culture fast enough."

"Culture, J.J.?" Crossnan said. "What is culture?"

"If you don't know what culture is, my boy, then I'm not going to waste
precious time telling you. I would remind you of what Thomas Davis said.
This country of ours is no sandbank thrown up by some recent caprice on
earth. It is an ancient land, honoured in the archives of civilization. The

man was right. This country had a culture by God, and they don't even know that down there."

Crossnan said, "They know what they know. And what they know is that what you call culture never put a penny in their pockets. Would you want them to be human museums, open all week, half-day Saturdays, so that we can all come and watch them?"

"Will you ever give over with that penny-in-your-pocket nonsense? There's no pricing culture."

Small crowds had gathered around the currachs, and from their vantage seat they watched the four hulls appear above the throng and move forward to the sea, seemingly under their own power, the legs of the men underneath hidden by the accompanying crowds.

—David Hanly

TRALEE

> She was lovely and fair
> As the rose of the summer
> But 'twas not her beauty alone
> That won me.
> Ah no, 'twas the love in her eyes
> Forever a dawning
> That made me love Mary
> The Rose of Tralee.
> —William Mulchinock

The capital of Kerry, gateway to the Dingle Peninsula, Tralee is a Georgian town of 13,000 souls known for its pleasant beaches and the Rose of Tralee Festival in September. At this time, amid much drinking and singing of ballads, the Rose is chosen. She and her court of beautiful runner-ups are then escorted to a ball by the most eligible of the young bachelors of Kerry—to dance the night away in the best of Kerry society.

If you fancy roses of the floral variety, you'll find a charming rose garden and a small memorial in the town park dedicated to William Mulchinock, the composer of the famous and much sentimentalized ballad "The Rose of Tralee."

LYNCHE'S OF THE SPA
5 miles out of Tralee on the Fenit road
Specialty: Seafood
In this pub there is almost always someone sitting at the piano, singing. The bar is extra-long and the seafood the best in the area.

For history buffs: St. Brendan the Navigator, credited in some circles with the discovery of America, was born in this neighborhood.

BALLYBUNION

If you're a bachelor and looking for an unusual experience, find out from the Irish Tourist Board what day in August will be Bachelor's Day in Ballybunion. Perhaps you'll be chosen the most eligible bachelor if you enter the contest. In any case, you'll enjoy the occasion and the contestants.

THE HARTY-COSTELLO PUB
Behind a nicely curving bar is friendly proprietor Jackie Hourigan, who assumes this position for four months of the year on top of his duties as a full-time veterinarian. Here you can learn something about both his quadruped and his biped customers.

When you've had enough of the drink, go down to the beach with its rugged cliffs, coves, and hidden caves.

LISTOWEL

Pronounced Lishtowel by Kerry people, this little town has become famous because of its affiliation with and special affection for writers. Native sons: George Fitzmaurice, who wrote for the early Abbey Theatre; Maurice Walsh, author of *The Quiet Man;* Bryan McMahon (*Children of the Rainbow*); and, most visibly, John B. Keane, who combines two outstanding Irish gifts by being both a writer and a publican.

John B., as he is affectionately referred to even by those who have never met him, is a prolific writer of books and plays. A controversial figure (some of the more snobbish literary types look down on him), he is beloved by many for his humor and his ability to depict the foibles and exact speech patterns of country folk with a compassionate irony that is, in itself, utterly Irish in character.

John B., a thin, dark-haired man with a long face, cares a great deal about writing and writers and the indigenous Irish culture and language. It is he who is responsible for loosing on Listowel a virtual blizzard of words in the form of Writers' Week.

Once a year, usually in July, the town of Listowel is utterly taken over by this event, in which swarms of writers and would-be scribes descend upon every available bed-and-breakfast, hotel, and pub to attend a giant series of conferences. There are poetry workshops and readings by the likes of Brendan Kennelly, Trinity College professor and poet. There are numerous awards, my favorite being the John Jameson Humourous Essay Open Competition. First prize in this competition is £150, plus a cut-glass decanter and a bottle of Jameson's whiskey (Joyce's favorite). This prize is considered appropriate for an Irish writer with wit.

There are musical events, plays, a book fair, an international poster exhibit, and of course endless parties, both spontaneous and official. Inevitably, as in any Irish gathering, there is a great deal of talk, gossip, and conjecture, in this case most of it exceptionally sharp and epigrammatic.

Television has made inroads into what is traditionally the writers' turf. Ulick O'Connor, a writer and TV personality (and the object of some pointed barbs from fellow journalists), was recognized in the simplest pub:

"I'm glad to see ya, Mr. Ulick," said a local man, turning from his pint. "I read your articles. Shaw and you are my favorites. Actually, Shaw is my favorite . . . I've got a story to tell ya sometime . . ."

"About Shaw?" asked the smiling Mr. O'Connor.

"No, about me." General laughter.

JOHN B. KEANE'S

John B. Keane, yes, he's Listowel's cottage industry.

—Name withheld upon request

The world around us, particularly the rural world, is alive with singing language and fabulous characters, but there's little respect for the country poet anymore. . . . Every townland and parish is vibrant with the ballads of our departed poets. They're waiting to be adopted and woven into the fabric of a living theatre, a theatre which is forcing its way upward and outward.

—John B. Keane

The above, written by the owner of this pub, tells you a great deal about the flavor of his establishment. Physically, it is an intimate place with the conversational gap between bar and tables easily bridged. The room is small enough that the arriving stranger might feel like an intruder upon entering, but don't be daunted—the natives are friendly after a brief interval.

I came to visit J.B.'s place on a day when the weather was what is euphemistically referred to in Kerry as "spiritual." A silvery drizzle dampened my hair as I walked along the streets discovering the nineteenth-century architectural delights peculiar to Listowel—stone sculptures over the doorways composed of lions, sunbursts, ladies, and birds.

In a wide street angling off to the left of Keane's, a horse fair was in progress. Ignoring the rain as all Irish country people do, a mingle of men of all ages lined the sides of the street. They watched with hooded interest as every now and again a horse gleaming and slick with rain was trotted past by his owner. Bargaining was so casual and low-key, so calm and conversational, it was hard to see it happen at all.

There were no writers here. They were all in workshops or pubs.

COUNTY LIMERICK

LIMERICK

Limerick cured ham and Limerick lace enjoy a worldwide reputation. The thousand-year-old city once drew Norse and English overlords; now it is a terminal for rail and sea traffic. There is something claustro-

phobic and dour about Limerick in spite of its location on the estuary of
Ireland's longest river, the Shannon.

Some points of interest in Limerick: spanning the river is Thomond
Bridge, with one end in County Clare and the other in Limerick. On
the Clare side is the explanation of why so many Irish bars are called
The Treaty Stone. On a pedestal is an irregular block of limestone said
to be the Treaty Stone on which the treaty of 1691 was signed. This
treaty is important in Irish memory because it gave full honors to the
brave Irish forces defending Limerick against William of Orange, even
though, after a long siege, they lost. Unfortunately, it was never rati-
fied. The Protestant parliament refused to legalize a treaty that guaranteed religious tolerance for Catholics.

On Bridge Street is the Gerald Griffin Memorial School, formerly
the old courthouse where the trial of John Scanlon took place for the
murder of his wife, Ellen. He was defended by Daniel O'Connell; but
even that great orator couldn't save him, and he was executed. The
story of this love-murder inspired a young Limerick reporter to write a
novel about it, *The Collegians*, which in turn became the basis for the
famous Boucicault drama *The Colleen Bawn*. Almost every man, woman, and child in Ireland can tell you the story, and will, at the drop of a
pint.

CHARLES ST. GEORGE'S
Across from the railway station

> I stand for an Irish civilization based on the people and embodying the
> things—their habits, their ways of thought, customs—that make them
> different—the sort of life that I was brought up in. . . . Once, years ago, a
> crowd of us were walking along the Shepherd's Bush Road [England] when
> out of a lane came a chap with a donkey—just the sort of donkey and just
> the sort of cart they have at home. He came out quite suddenly and
> abruptly and we all cheered him. Nobody who has not been an exile will
> understand me, but I stand for that.
>
> —Michael Collins

Charlie St. George is a white-haired man getting on in years but still
full of vigor. There is humor, too, in the lines of his thin, slightly stern
face.

Charlie's place is a workingman's pub, a favorite of several Irish writers and well known to most rugby players. It is a "Patriots" pub and reflects Charlie, himself an ex-rugby player (wing forward) and ardent republican.

The pub is long and dark, with the bar taking up most of the space. The walls are a veritable museum, covered with old photos, yellowing playbills, portraits, paintings, and sayings.

Pint in hand, listening to Charlie's comments, I browsed among the mementos: a Parnell poster dated 1912; a portrait of Sean O'Casey rescued from the fire at the old Abbey Theatre (page 70) and given to Charlie by an actor; the Belvedere hurling team in 1919; Charlie himself in 1927, in his striped rugby shirt.

I looked closely at the photo of Michael Collins, the handsome patriot-rebel known as "the Big Fellow," and "the Laughing Boy." Along with Eamon De Valera, Collins took up arms against the Anglo-Irish treaty of 1921, which partitioned Ireland and, though it established an Irish Free State, did not create a united Ireland.

Collins was killed in the ensuing civil war—ambushed in a valley called Beal Na Blath or "Valley (Gap) of the Flowers." Michael Collins was himself a flower of Irish manhood—young, brilliant, impassioned, and articulate—and his death is in the tradition, almost poetic, of the Irish martyr-hero.

Martyrs certainly hold a place of great importance in Irish history and in Irish hearts. The Irish American Richard Brown once told me that Ireland is for him a metaphor for the human condition. For society, it seems, martyrs are a part of the process of change.

Originally, the Easter Uprising of 1916 was a failure—the people were not behind it. But in executing this small band of dedicated revolutionaries, the English transformed them into martyrs, thus enraging the Irish and inspiring them to rally behind their fallen compatriots. So it was the English themselves who gave the Irish the heroes they needed for success in the struggle for independence. Perhaps those who "rose" were not unaware of the possibility of this outcome.

At the photo of a group of dark-suited men, Charlie St. George stopped and said in a voice still vibrant with outrage, "That's the Murder Gang." This was the name given to Dublin Castle's secret service agents—those men who hunted and killed members of the IRA. "And here's Sean Treacy," Charlie continued, "the greatest fighter ever lived."

It is a ritual, a vestige of an oral tradition, this emotional remembering—a key to keeping alive the deeply rooted Irish sense of clan loyalty that is at once proud and stifling.

From Sean Treacy we moved to the Belvedere hurling team. Hurling, too, is a part of Ireland's tradition of the heroic—according to legend, men were hurling in Ireland when the gods of Greece were still young (unlike sex, which, an Irish wag claims, "is still in its infancy here"). The great mythic hero Cuchulainn was a champion hurler, and no hero of old was worth a Celtic damn if he couldn't expertly wield the four-foot, bronze-bound, ash caman to drive the fist-sized hurling ball. Today, hurling is still popular in the south. However, the sport has had to give ground to Gaelic football and rugby.

From the end of the bar a group of hefty young men had been watching my progress around the room. I soon found myself in the midst of these friendly athletes, being plied with pints and information.

Gaelic football is a community game played throughout Ireland, while rugby (brought to Ireland only in 1850 by the English) draws its players from the ranks of white-collar workers and students in secondary schools and universities.

Gaelic football is played from September through April. International matches draw enormous crowds (60,000–70,000) of passionate and vocal partisans. So important is football that it even crowds news off the front page of the venerable Irish Times. Intercounty competitions draw fanatic followings, with the brawny men of Kerry winning the most consistently, perhaps in retribution for the "Kerryman jokes," the Irish version of the "idiot joke" that every country has. Sample: "Did ya hear the one about two Kerrymen who were lost in the desert on the day of the All Ireland Football Final—with tongues hanging out and the remorseless sun beating down, one turns to the other and says, 'Thank God, it's a great day for the match anyway.' "

If you're around for the match between Cork and Kerry (in Dublin), go. The ancient feud between the two cities really finds expression there.

SOUTH'S
Top of O'Connell Street

This is a timeless old pub with a tranquillity akin to what you feel when looking at a painting of a Dutch interior. The floor is checkerboard black-and-white and the partitioned bar a cool white marble. When you sit down, its height is remarkable, reaching to chest level, and your glass is so close to your lips you barely need to raise it.

The wall behind the bar is a Victorian elaboration of curved mahogany arches framing bottles and old, painted mirrors. *John Jameson & Sons Old Malt* proclaims one mirror. Beneath the old-fashioned lettering are those hallmarks of Ireland: the greyhound, the harp, the castle, and the round tower.

To the side is a snug with walls of milk glass, and on the bulletin board in the rather more casual back room is a photographic roster of star rugby players. Behind this room is the back back room, graced with a skylight and hunting tapestries.

I had heard that South's pours the best Guinness in town, and I can certainly recommend it. As I sat at the bar applying my own taste test to the brew, I gazed up at the coffered ceiling and tuned in on the conversation of two old men at a table behind me. It was all place names and family connections:

"John Daly was in yesterday . . ."

"John Daly? Now, would he be from Killarney?"

"No, that's Margaret O'Connor's boy you're tinkin' of."

"Margaret O'Connor? Her father came from Cork . . ." etc., etc.

The most common question a stranger is asked when entering a pub is "Where are ye from?" In Ireland this question is more than just curiosity. Here people identify closely with their home ground: they feel a bond with the corners of Ireland that "reared them up." Finding out where someone comes from is finding out who they are: each family name is associated with a specific region, i.e., O'Flannery with Limerick.

IRISH COFFEE

It has been said that one Irish coffee is enough, two is too many, and three not half enough. Unlike whiskey, which was discovered by the Irish well before A.D. 1178, Irish coffee is a recent invention. Its tasty advent is credited to Joe Sheridan, one-time chef at Shannon Airport. Here follow instructions on the ceremony and preparation of this modern Irish contribution to the world's pleasures:

The Official Formula

Warm a stemmed glass. Put into it a generous jigger of Bushmills whiskey, sugar to taste, and hot, strong, black coffee. Pour pure, fresh cream very slightly whipped (*never* commit the sin of using the aerated-can stuff) onto the top. To make sure that the cream floats gently on the surface of the coffee, it is a good idea to place a turned-over spoon at the edge of the glass just above the coffee line. Then pour the cream gently over the spoon until it rests lightly on top of the coffee mixture.

Sip the result and join the connoisseurs who revel in the contrasting textures and temperatures when the cool cream touches the upper lip and the mouth is filled with hot whiskey-coffee.

Remember: Irish coffee must be made with *Irish* whiskey and *pure* cream.

ADARE

In 1976 Adare won first place in Ireland's National Tidy Towns competition. And no wonder. Driving into this town of 500 or so people is like entering one of those perfect little medieval towns pictured in children's books. Adare—even the name is lovely—means Ford of Oaks.

Along the banks of the river Maigue, in a rich and quiet setting, are thatched cottages; timbered black-and-white houses; and many romantic ruins and lichen-covered churches. There is a nine-hole golf course, fishing in the river—salmon, trout, and course fish. Course fishing is free; for salmon and trout, a license is available from July to September.

You can follow the hounds from October to March, and the woods

THATCHING

There are 947 registered thatched dwellings in the Republic of Ireland. To correct this disproportion and to instill a new interest in thatching, the Irish government has started a training program at the Craggaunowen Project. Patty O'Neill is the master teacher here, passing his craft on to young people.

"If you've ever lived inside a drum, you'd know what it's like to live under a tin roof with the raindrops pelting on it. But under a thatched roof, there is no sound; it is soft, like rain on a cushion," says Patty.

The material used for thatching—reeds and rushes—is harvested from the rivers in winter; then cut, stacked, and left to dry. The stacks are in bundles three feet long. In the summer and spring it is hauled and thatched.

Just before the bundles are arranged on the roof—12 inches apart in ascending order—the reeds are stumped against the ground several times to make them watertight and to give the roof a finished look.

are full of game if you like less formal hunting—grouse, pheasant, snipe, woodcock, and duck. For information, inquire at the local sporting-goods store.

The village dates from the Norman conquest, but it owes its wide, shady main street and charming appearance to the third Earl of Dunraven, who designed and laid it out in the nineteenth century. His house and grounds, Adare Manor, are open to the public from May to December.

The eighteenth-century poet Sean O'Tuoma kept hens at Adare Manor for the lady of the manor. This was after he had run a pub he owned into bankruptcy. A generous and gregarious man, he advertised free tankards of ale to any fellow poet; it turned out, there were quite a number of thirsty poets in the area. He was literally quaffed out of his pub, but not before he and his literary cronies had invented the art of the limerick. In honor of this gift to the world, every May there is a festival called *Fielena Maighue* in the towns in the Maigue district, commemorating Sean and his pub.

COLLINS'

This timbered pub has been modernized, but subtly and in keeping with the general architectural quality of the whole town. The dark-beamed ceiling, white walls, and red furnishings contrast pleasantly.

Collins' is used for many functions, like weddings; maybe you'll run into a party.

After leaving Collins' I drove along Main Street intending to leave town, but a sign caught my eye: HERBAL MEDICINE. I had heard a good bit about Irish "country cures," so I pulled over to investigate.

The herbalist lived in a small thatched cottage snuggled behind thick yew hedges. An elderly, heavy-set man in shapeless brown pants and suspenders opened a low door and ushered me into his consultation room. This room was a back parlor crammed with plants, old tea cups, boxes, holy pictures, machine parts, roots hanging from the ceiling, and several ancient wooden chairs with the paint peeling. Here he made me a cup of tea on a hot plate and began chatting companionably about my life. He was gathering rather than taking my medical history.

When asked about his herbal remedies, he smiled and changed the subject. He wasn't going to give away his secrets. "I see people from many miles around," he said. "Even foreigners like yourself come to me. I help them." He paused, smiled again, and said, "To be honest wit ya, there's nothin wrong wit ye atall."

Here are a few Irish pishrogues or country superstitions:

Spiderwebs are good for cuts.

The inside of a marrowbone rubbed onto the affected area will cure baldness.

Spittle rubbed onto warts after a wake will cure them.

A man named O'Sullivan can cure the gout.

Drink a pint jug of your own urine to cure jaundice.

Moss from a human skull will close an open wound.

Potatoes at the bottom of the bed will ward off rheumatism.

COUNTY CLARE

DURTY NELLIE'S
On the Limerick road
Next to Bunratty Castle (7 miles from Shannon Airport)
Food: Full menu, excellent smoked salmon

Durty Nellie's is a great favorite with native and tourist alike and is always "packed out" cheek by jowl. The pub is a ramshackle old cottage with a thatched roof, sitting like some outrageous upstart at the foot of the monolithic Bunratty Castle. The fact that it has been somewhat commercialized is no matter—the place is sheer fun.

It is a warren of small rooms, little bars, cozy fireplace seats, innumerable nooks and crannies. The walls are covered with historical artifacts, portraits of martyrs and statesmen and their writings. Look at the walls and you'll get a short course in Irish history.

Durty Nellie's is borderline "twee" (self-consciously quaint) but manages not to fall on the wrong side of the border. The furniture and setting, in keeping with a tavern of the seventeenth century, are somehow truly charming.

The downstairs is always crowded to bursting with jolly people, and the ensuing din is interlaced with the strains of impromptu music. You can addle yourself with a combination of Guinness and music by straddling the doorway between two rooms and attempting to listen to the music in each.

At the top of the narrow wooden staircase is a surprise—a kind of glassed-in cage containing birds flitting among attractively arranged branches. This peaceful motif is echoed in the atmosphere upstairs; much quieter, a good place for a tête-à-tête, with its low ceiling and small old-fashioned windows.

When you grow tired of the noise and smoke, take your pint and sit outside on the small veranda or wander a few feet to the stone bridge that arches over the Shannon. I can't guarantee it, but one of the high points in your tour of Irish pubs just might be standing on the bridge with the moon rising over the river and Bunratty Castle, floodlit and imposing, on your left. Sounds of music and laughter float out of the windows of the pub. The air is soft and still, and evening birds swoop over all.

One of the most inspired aspects of the out-of-town Irish pub is the free flow between indoors and out. To emerge from the talk and dim cramp into the mellow smells and sights of an Irish evening is to delight the heart. Then, after dawdling in the luminous hush, you can duck back in refreshed and ready for another round.

Food here is first-rate (several stars to the salmon salad), but if you're eating, be sure to make a reservation. Or, if you want a banquet, go next door to Bunratty Castle, where they feature a true medieval feast every night, complete with music and costumed waiters and waitresses.

NEWMARKET ON FERGUS

BELSFORT INN

Belsfort is a new pub, a cross between a roadhouse and a pub. Its decor is dimly comfortable, with stained glass, stained wood, and discreet plastic. It is the pub's location that makes it interesting, standing as it does beside a fairy ring.

Until very recently the culture of Ireland was the culture of the countryside. It was densely populated by supernatural beings: *leprechauns*, solitary shoemakers; *gancanaghs*, seducers of milkmaids; *far darrigs*, first-class practical jokers; *pookas*, birds or beasts who take the unwary on wild night rides; *dullahans*, headless messengers of death; *lean shees*, who inspire poets and musicians; *banshees*, who keen and wail at the death of a loved one. And these are only a few.

Historians suggest that the fairies were the gods of pagan, Celtic Ireland. Mixing Christianity with pagan lore produced the belief that the fairies were fallen angels not good enough to be taken back into Heaven, but not bad enough to be sent in the other direction. Cultural anthropologists trace the origin of the fairies back to the mythic battle for Ireland between the Tuatha De Danaan, the original inhabitants, and the invading Celts. The Tuatha De Danaan were vanquished, but they were greatly revered by their conquerors for their mastery of magic and of many other arts. After their defeat, the Tuatha De Danaan retreated into earthen mounds, called *sid*, and become the *sidhe*, or fairy people.

There are hundreds of folktales involving the doings of the fairies. W. B.
Yeats, perhaps Ireland's greatest poet, studied them, understood their value, and attempted to preserve them. He wrote: "These folk tales are full of
simplicity and musical occurrences, for they are the literature of a class for
whom every incident in the old rut of birth, love, pain and death has
cropped up unchanged for centuries: who have steeped everything in the
heart: to whom everything is a symbol.

I don't believe in fairies even if they do exist.

—Anonymous Irishman

MILLTOWN MALBAY

I arrived in Milltown Malbay under the worst and best possible circumstances. It was pouring rain and it was the week in July when this little
town becomes a center for all truly devoted practitioners of Irish traditional music, with the emphasis on piping.

My companions were three young Dubliners who brought with them
a wide assortment of jokes, a guitar, and a set of Uilleann pipes. We
parked at the end of a line of cars that stretched ever farther out of town
as new devotees continued to arrive.

Annually, in July, the entire county of Clare becomes one giant music festival. A few miles up the coast, Lisdoonvarna was hosting 20,000
fans—the musicians had well-known names (The Chieftains, Emmy-
lou Harris), but my friends assured me that the "real crack" would be
here in Milltown Malbay. (They must have been right—I saw a member of The Chieftains in a local restaurant. He had snuck away from the
big doings for a secret hour here among the "cognoscenti.")

Milltown Malbay is the birthplace of the great piper Willy Clancy,
and the festival here is a kind of fraternity party for pipers from all over
the world. Aside from nonstop (literally) music and talk, there are
workshops at which you can learn not only how to play but also how to
make pipes.

And where is the music played? Yes, of course—in the pubs. The
musicians move from one pub to another all afternoon and deep into
the night, switching venue for fresh inspiration and playing partners.
The visitor to Milltown Malbay will do best by following their example.

As I made the rounds of the pubs with my friends, time stopped and the experience became a mélange of music and pints shot through with talk and laughter.

The musicians are a bizarre mixture of types and nationalities: "auld fellas" whose skills are legendary, yet who make music as naturally as they plant fields; long-haired youngsters with intense faces who grow tired and drunk and fall asleep under the tables and on the benches; woolly-sweatered girls in long skirts; strait-laced intellectuals; shambling students wearing American University T-shirts; ordinary people from the Irish countryside. Some of these are magicians who can play you into a trance, others are there to learn.

The pubs are full of people from miles around: families, children, and local people clap, sing, and celebrate.

Officially the pubs close at 11:30. Actually, what this means is that the doors are locked at 11:30. No one may enter, and those who leave will not be permitted back. Behind the locked doors a mood of intimacy sets in, the publican brings out refreshments, and the true musicians hit their stride. It is wise, therefore, to make a quick tour of the pubs before 11:30 to make sure you'll be in the right spot to hear the best music when the clock strikes closing time.

The unlucky ones who forget are left standing outside and try every means to get in. They crowd around the locked doors knocking, and when the barman opens up a crack, they employ every device known to the inventive Irish mind to weave stories that will allow them in. The beleaguered barman rewards one or two with the best stories by letting them slip through the conspiratorially half-open door.

One of my companions was caught outside at 11:30 and told the publican that he absolutely had to gain entry because his girlfriend was inside and he felt an intense urge to propose marriage to her that very instant. He didn't make it, though his story provided a good laugh for the crowd inside. I glanced at his girlfriend; she seemed to think it funniest of all . . . yet after a while, grumbling, she went out to join him, causing even more hilarity and bawdy comment.

Finally, at 3:00 a.m., the publicans closed up shop, but the musicians kept going until dawn.

When we came out of our pub, a thin moon shone on the squat stone houses. The crowd milled about under the streetlight in front of the pub; then a tin whistle took up a reel, the notes clear and flowing as an

upland stream. People crowded around the player, and upstairs the publican's children, who had just finished collecting the glasses for their
father, leaned out to listen. "That's Mary Bergen playing," whispered
my Dublin friend; "she's the best in the land." After a bewitching few
moments, Mary was joined by a guitar and fiddle, and as I walked away,
people old and young had begun to dance the Irish polka, illuminated
by the pale moon and the circle of light from the street lamp.

A minute later I was in the total darkness of the sweet-smelling Irish
night, driving through fields toward the sea.

A *word of caution:* You must either be prepared to not sleep at all, to
sleep in your car, or to make advance reservations for lodging during
this festival. The best way to do this is through the Irish Tourist Board.
Better yet, arrive several days early and spend some time exploring the
coast and the famous inland area known as the Burren.

LAHINCH

Lahinch is a resort town at the water's edge. At the outskirts of the
village colorful tents dot the cliff edge, where campers fall asleep to the
sound of the sea. The surf is high on perfect beaches, always within
reach at the end of every little crooked lane. A serious golf course, one
of the best in Ireland, stretches out beside the sea. Though the town is
composed of the usual stone houses, its position by the sea somehow
gives it a Mediterranean flavor.

MULCHAHY'S

This pub, housed in a building over a century old, has been renovated,
but nicely so. The floor is flagstone, the walls timbered and whitewashed. There is traditional and show music nightly.

Spend the evening in Mulchahy's, and early the next day drive north
a few miles along the coast road through the little fishing village of Lis-
cannor to the Cliffs of Moher, rising a dramatic 700 feet from the sea.
Take the windy, winding cliff walk to the lookout in O'Brien's Tower
and "hang your head over, hear the wind blow." This lonely old tower

is a romantic landmark, small as the human presence against the might of cliffs, sky, and sea. It was placed there by the O'Briens, the family that once ruled the area in the days of feuding clans and crenellated castles.

From this perch atop the cliffs you can see the west coast from Kerry to Connemara. The famous Moher flagstones are quarried near here. In former times a bride's dowry often consisted of "Moher flags," which provided a floor for many a humble kitchen. This stone is still in great demand for flooring and fireplaces.

Head inland to Lisdoonvarna, Ireland's premier spa. The principal sulphur spring is at the south side of town, the principal iron spring at the north side. At the Spa Center you will find all the facilities for a renewed you, from baths to sauna and massage.

Five miles from Lisdoonvarna is Doolin Cove, where boats may be hired to take you to the Aran Islands. Doolin is basically a grocery store and pub.

DOOLIN

O'CONNOR'S

O'Connor's has earned an international reputation as a mecca for traditional music. The place has been in the O'Connor family since 1832, and the present Mr. O'Connor is very friendly. Five families, he told me, still live in Doolin Cove, where they survive by carrying on the tradition of lobster fishing.

In the front is the usual small Irish grocery store with a tiny counter and shelves crammed with everything from Galtee cheese to gloves.

The extensions in the back have been added on over the years. The main room is blessed with a fireplace for cold, misty days, and on the walls are dozens of photographs of the musicians who play here, of fishermen, of Irish faces and Irish life.

The music is not organized—the sessions are spontaneous, occurring night and day, whenever the musicians choose to drop in. Sandwiches and coffee are available (besides pints), but no one minds if you go out front, buy your bit of cheese, ham, and tomatoes, and eat your purchase then and there at one of the tables. The crowd is local-international;

rucksacks and young faces abound. The following description of O'Connor's appeared in *The New York Times*, February 17, 1974. Nothing has changed at the present writing.

The body space available to each individual was roughly that found in a New York subway crush. Fortunately, once we had pushed into the interior of the pub, we discovered that the door to the room where the draft kegs were kept was open and cool air washed in from the sea; we hovered in the doorway, found it was possible to make an occasional foray into the bar for a pint, sip it in the semi-seclusion of the keg room, and still listen to the three musicians. All were in their seventies.

The music was related to our own Bluegrass, the fiddle lively and plaintive by turn, the piper spirited, the drummer persistent. Occasionally, it even reminded me of Baroque music. The sound was absorbed within twenty feet of the trio by a willing audience: the others in the pub talked and smoked and drank. In the air-cooled back room there were scores of aluminum kegs, a dozen of which were attached by transparent plastic tubing that went through the wall to the appropriate taps at the bar some 50 feet away. Periodically, a man came from the bar, exchanged a full barrel for an empty, tapping the new keg. A quarter-twist to disconnect the siphon top center, then a quarter-twist in the opposite direction to affix the tubing to the fresh keg.

—Edwin Miller

THE BURREN
BALLYVAUGHAN

Not a tree whereon to hang a man; no water in which to drown him; no soil in which to bury him.

—Anonymous

Stony seabord, far and foreign,
    Stony hills poured over space,
Stony outcrop of the Burren,
    Stones in every fertile place,
Little fields with boulders dotted,
Grey-stone shoulders saffron-spotted,
Stone-walled cabins thatched with reeds,

Where a Stone Age people breeds
The last of Europe's stoneage race.
—John Betjeman
"Sunday in Ireland"

Inland from Ballyvaughan, Lisdoonvarna, and Lahinch is the hundred or so square mile area known as the Burren, a word meaning rock. It is a place of mystery, a strange lunarlike landscape frozen forever in carboniferous limestone, speaking the language of the Neolithic past.

Ireland is unique in containing many such spots, physically varied, yet all emitting an intense, eerie, primordial spirit. The relics scattered at these sites tell a moving story of man's early history and of his ties to Mother Earth.

The Burren is a rarity in itself; but when you explore it, you will find above and below its scarred surface even more extraordinary rarities.

In early summer this desert literally blooms with thousands of the fairest and rarest flowers on earth, turning particularly the northern part near Ballyvaughan into a veritable rock garden. The presence of these primarily arctic and alpine blooms in this alien area remains a botanical mystery.

There are many active cave systems in the Burren, but they have not been commercially developed and you should have had some spelunking experience if you want to explore them. The most spectacular is in Pollnagollum: seven miles of surveyed cave complete with a 250-foot waterfall. Near Ballynadocken, on the south side of Slieve Elva, is a cave with the world's largest stalactite, 20 feet. (They're the ones that hang down. I've always remembered the difference between stalactite and stalagmite by the little saying: "When the mites go up, the tites come down.")

Amazingly, this barren area was once well populated, as the great number of stone circles, megalithic tombs, and cairns bear out. Literally, you can hardly avoid stumbling on a stone fort—there are 700 of them.

Less than five miles south of Ballyvaughan on the road to Corofin is the Paulnabrone Dolmen, its stone form blending harmoniously into the environment. Formerly it was thought that these prehistoric grave memorials, so like giant stone tables, were altars used by the Druids.

There *is* something haunting about these ancient ceremonial sculptures.

Actually, the entire Burren area is haunted—by history and legend. The many ruined castles have made Clare's reputation as "the county of castles." There is even a ghost, a former inhabitant of Leamanch Castle, that walks the area. She is Maire Ruadh, the wife of Connor O'Brien:

> She was riding her black stallion to Limerick, and she passed a poor miserable house on the roadside. She said it offended her, and it was to be thrown down before she came back that way. So the poor woman that lived in the house came out and looked after the great lady and the black horse. Then she fell on her bare knees on the road and she cursed Maire Ruadh, that she might never ride back that way. So, as the lady and the black horse went through the woods at Cratloe, there came a great wind, and the branch of a tree came down and it caught Maire by the throat, and her neck was broken and she died. So the living woman never rode back that way. . . . But of a stormy night you'll hear the heavy feet of the stallion, and him galloping the road up to Leamanch.
>
> *Ireland—The Burren Region* (Midwestern regional tourism pamphlet)

Another legend involves St. Colman, to whom are dedicated no less than three churches in the Burren, two of these extremely old. St. Colman made his hermitage on the slopes of Slieve Carran, where he lived with a servant and three pets: a cock to crow at the times for prayer, a mouse to waken him from sleep, and a fly to follow the lines of the book he was reading and mark his place should he be interrupted and have to return to it later.

The legend is about Colman and his half-brother King Guaire, who lived in Kinvara in neighboring Galway (you can visit Guaire Castle there). It was the end of Lent, the story goes, and St. Colman and his servant had no food with which to break their long penitential fast. Colman felt sorry for his servant (being a saint he probably didn't mind so much for himself). King Guaire, meanwhile, was feasting merrily with a few friends several miles away.

For the sake of his servant, the saint caused the steaming dishes to rise from the table and fly over the hills to the hermitage. The guests, quite understandably, were astonished and fascinated and, quickly mounting their horses, followed the plates on their journey to the hermitage. On arriving, the King was overjoyed to find his half-brother and promptly built him a monastery, which today is called Kilmac-duagh, said to date back to 610. There are some who say that if you follow the trail of the dishes (known as Bothea na Mios), you can still see the brown stains of the gravy that spilled from the airborne dinner as it flew to its destination. If you are patient and diligent, you can find the ruins of the hermitage in the tangle of trees and underbrush.

These monuments to Colman stand in a hollow below the famous Abbey of Corcomroe, a twelfth-century Cistercian foundation of which only the church still stands. Its old name was St. Mary-of-the-Fertile-Rock, and as the name suggests, the church is a fruitful combination of pagan and Christian sensibilities set in a lush green cleft between two limestone mountains. The capitals of the columns in the choir and transept chapels are a hymn to life, carved with human faces, leaves, berries, and acorns.

It is in the hills around this abbey that Yeats set the action for his play *The Dreaming of the Bones,* a title that beautifully captures the spirit of the Burren.

O'LOCHLAIN'S PUB

This is a very small, very clean, very neat pub in the front room of a whitewashed 200-year-old house. The floor is swept stone, and there are a few benches and small tables. At the bar are several old gentlemen in greatcoats and caps. They drink their tranquil pints while the inlaid wooden wall clock ticks away, as it has since 1890.

If you ask, you can see the visitors' book, which has comments and wry remarks dating back to 1870. When you leave, the owner will ring up your bill on the ornate nineteenth-century till that somehow found its way to Ireland from Dayton, Ohio.

O'Lochlain is the name of a family once powerful in this corner of the Burren; one of their castles, Gleninagh, abandoned only a generation ago, still commands the shore near Black Head. Its generous fireplace brings to mind the feasting and fighting of days gone by.

ENNISTYMON

Ennistymon is a holiday center about two miles inland from Lahinch. It is situated in a wooded valley beside a cascade on the river Cullenagh, where, if you're an angler, you'll be made happy by the excellent brown trout.

VAUGHN'S PUB
Main Street
A tiny old pub run by Lily Vaughn, whose way with words has won her a brisk clientele. Quite a few country pubs traditionally have been run by women, and though, in the old days, women did not generally patronize pubs, there were exceptions. In *Letters of an Irish Publican* John B. Keane relates:

> Nowadays it is common for women to patronize pubs but when I was a young fellow it was out of the question. Not so with Cunnacanewer women or indeed those from other country townlands. They always drank with their men, mostly halves of hot porter or whiskey. Their shawlies or poorer women who were not as well off as the farmers' wives, would drink mulled porter the round of a Friday which is market day in Knockamee as well as being pension day. It is the busiest day of the week outside the high season time. They are well-behaved in the pub and apart from spitting on the floor, spilling an occasional drink, or puking without warning, are model customers. Now and then they argue, and on rare occasions they fight.

COUNTY TIPPERARY

County Tipperary, or "Tip," as it is fondly referred to by the natives, is Ireland's largest inland county. Its beauty is rich and varied—mountains, rivers, plains, and valleys. Tipperary lies in the fertile Golden Vale and is a dairy center. Horses are important in all of Ireland, but here in Tip, as in Meath, Limerick, and Kildare, they are a business as well as a passion. These counties are the principal breeding areas in Ireland; the grass is green and nourishing all year round, the water is laced with minerals that promote strong bones, the climate is mild.

TIPPERARY

Tip town, a dairy farming center north of the Sleivenamuck Hills, had its beginnings at the end of the twelfth century, when King John built a castle here and established Anglo-Norman rule.

The area figured prominently in the Land League agitation of the late nineteenth century, a grass-roots reform movement. Its method, as Conor and Maire Cruise O'Brien have written, was "to select estates especially notorious for rack-renting and eviction: concentrate public attention on those estates by means of mass meetings and then, by pressure of social ostracism, and refusal of services, render life as difficult as possible for the landlord (if resident) or his agent, and especially for 'grabbers'—those who rented land from which previous tenants had been evicted and which the Land League had placed under ban."

The power of the Anglo-Irish Ascendancy has disappeared, but a few of their traditions have found their way into Irish life: this is hunt country, and the famous Scarteen Black and Tans (foxhounds not people) tally-ho in this district.

The Anglo-Irish gentry are a very peculiar group of people these days. They are as powerless as any aristocracy in Europe, and yet in many ways they have not changed at all since the 18th century. Some of them still live in castles and Georgian houses—the architectural treasures of Ireland—built by their ancestors, and they still farm the land as their ancestors did. They grow barley, graze sheep and breed cattle or horses. Apart from agriculture, their vocation is war, or it was until the Suez crisis. Their avocations are blood sports—fox hunting, pheasant shooting—and salmon fishing. Few of them are rich anymore, so they live in many ways like all Irish farmers, doing the labor themselves, and burning peat or coal in the winter.

—Frances FitzGerald

TIDGE MOLONEY'S
Davis Street
A gem of an utterly plain Irish small-town pub—no snugs, no antiques,

but a whole wall of postcards, some yellowed with age, some scenic, some ribald, some unusual.

I was taken there as a first stop on a pub crawl by an old pony-trekking guide who befriended me. He was at once courtly and slyly sexual, as most Irish men are with foreign women. At first, half of his conversation completely passed me by, between his heavy brogue and his missing teeth; but after a few pints the language barrier seemed of no particular importance and was easily overcome by laughter.

O'DEA'S

Our last stop was O'Dea's. I think it is on the road from Tipperary to Lattin, but the night was dark and we *had* made a few stops on the way that fuzzed my accuracy somewhat. All I can say is if you want to be sure, ask for directions at Tidge Moloney's.

We made our way there through winding lanes and under a dark canopy of shadowy trees. When we arrived, the place was closed; my friend delivered a series of syncopated raps on the door, softly calling out his name. Turf smoke rose from the chimney, and the place gave out an aura of ancient comfort.

The door opened to reveal a band of pipe-smoking, becapped old men, and my friend gleefully introduced me as his cousin from New York. The bar was a narrow wooden counter behind which was the usual assortment of canned goods, candies, potato chips . . . Some of the cans had reached the status of antiques.

The old men tried to catch us out on our pseudo-relationship, and this involved much laughter. After a while I asked for the ladies' room, a request greeted with knowing smiles. A door was pointed out to me, and I found myself standing in the moonlight in a graveyard gazing upon the dim shapes of the Galtee Mountains.

"Now," said my friend when I returned, "you can tell them back home, 'I drank in a pub, I pissed in a graveyard and I looked at the Galtee Mountains all at the same time.' "

LOUGH DERG

Lough Derg, surrounded by lonely moors and heathery hills, is famous for the yearly pilgrimage to Station Island. St. Patrick is said to have spent forty days of solitary prayer in a cave on this island before finally expelling the evil spirits that infested it. Today, only pilgrims are allowed on this island for an arduous three days of fasting and barefoot penitence.

Don't be put off, however, by this austere footnote. Lough Derg offers much more than the memory of a saintly struggle.

PADDY'S PUB (Terryglass) / SAIL INN (Dromineer)
Terryglass

If you love to fish or just to take a leisurely ride on a lake cruiser, there are two exceptionally delightful pubs on the shores of Lough Derg that come highly recommended by the Irish writer and wit Hugh Leonard:

> There is an extra pleasure in sighting a distant pub from the bridge of a lake cruiser. You can't quite spot Paddy's Pub in Terryglass as you approach the tiny harbour in the northeast corner of Lough Derg: it is a short walk up a winding lane, and you are no sooner in this tiny hamlet than out of it. The pub is small, dark and a jewel of its kind. The other lake pub is the Sail Inn at Dromineer, 90 minutes cruising time south of Terryglass. It is part of a splendid inn and restaurant run by a daunting English lady—or Lady, rather, since she is titled. I myself had the honour of declaring the new bar open, and the view from its balcony is enchanting.

CASHEL

> *On the grey Rock of Cashel I suddenly saw*
> *A Sphinx with woman breast and lion paw,*
> *A Buddha, hand at rest,*
> *Hand lifted up that blest.*
> —W. B. Yeats

The Rock is, in all truth, a vision, seen either in the detail of arches and tower and old carven stone, or seen suddenly and startlingly from a distance. No one will ever forget his first prospect of the Rock of Cashel. For most of us, including myself, it comes on the road from Dublin to the south, or to Cork. . . .

The road ascends a gentle slope and takes an easy curve and there it is, not just a rock but a fantastic stranded ship, the original limestone that came up out of the fertile clay now horned and crowned with the accretions of the centuries—some of them of surprising architectural beauty, some of them creatures of fantasy like the crazily-elongated Celtic cross that a vain man set sailing like a mast above his family tomb.

—Benedict Kiely

As you can imagine from Ben Kiely's lyric description, Cashel is one of Ireland's most spectacular sights. It is as though Ireland herself gathered the geology, history, and culture of the land into one outcropping, creating a place full of mysterious, brooding force, even in brilliant sunshine.

Standing atop this powerful landmark, you are treated to a stunning view of the surrounding countryside. Distant mountains rise from the Golden Vale: the blue shapes of Slievenaman, the Knockmealdowns, the Comeraghs, and the Galtees. The landscape shifts under cloud-shadow and comes alive in the constantly changing light that is one of Ireland's major miracles.

The Rock has been meaningful in Irish history for some 1,500 years; and tradition designates it as the ancient home of the immortals, the Tuatha De Danaan. Cashel was the seat of the Munster kings from around 370 to 1101, when King Murtagh O'Brien granted it to the Church, turning the Rock into a great power center where temporal and ecclesiastic rule conjoined.

In the centuries to follow, it became a sometimes bizarre bellwether of Ireland's fortunes, first as a center for culture and then, at the end of the sixteenth century, falling upon lean times with the impact of the Reformation. In 1495, Gerald, Earl of Kildare, burned the cathedral down because, as he explained, he thought the archbishop was inside.

In the following century, Cromwell's troops did not spare Cashel: in a mindless and horrific bloodbath they murdered 3,000 townspeople who had taken refuge there. Their rampage also caused the destruction of many sacred images and the breaking up of the great crucifix.

In 1749 Protestant Archbishop Agar committed the final outrage by unroofing the great cathedral and opening it to the wind and weather. Still, it abides, its massive skeletal remains wedded to the rock upon which it stands.

And upon this rock also stood Ireland's favorite and patron saint, Patrick, from whom every second male child gets his name. On visiting Cashel in 450 B.C., St. Patrick baptized King Aengus on the spot where the high cross now stands, creating the first Christian monarch of the Rock. During the ceremony, Patrick accidentally stuck his famous crosier into the foot of the King, but the proud warrior, unacquainted with his new religion, stood silently and bore the pain, thinking it a part of the initiation ceremony.

Some say it was on Cashel that the good saint picked the shamrock (bringing instant fame to the little, ubiquitous Irish clover) to demonstrate the mystery of the Trinity. But should you claim this honor for Cashel in other parts of Ireland, you may open the door to immediate controversy. The Irish are in agreement on only one thing regarding the shamrock and the saint: he picked it, and he picked it in Ireland.

THE KING
Dublin–Cork road (just on the Dublin side of Cashel)
Food: Full menu
This is a modern hotel built in a hexagonal form. The glassed-in pub area commands a truly astounding view of the Rock and the surrounding countryside.

Lunches are quite good, especially the roast beef and the trout. Pub grub is pleasantly served, and the sandwiches are very fresh.

CONNAUGHT

County Galway   County Roscommon

County Mayo   County Leitrim

County Sligo

COUNTY GALWAY

GALWAY

Galway is billed as the "Gateway to the West," and so it is—a funnel through which you pass to the enormous solitude of Connemara and the heart of the western Gaeltacht.

It is generally agreed that the Bay of Galway was the "Ausoba" of Ptolemy, the second-century Egyptian geographer who apparently identified the city as Magnata or Nagata. In 1232, when Richard de Burgh took over, Galway became a flourishing Anglo-Norman colony, home of the Fourteen Tribes of Galway. These were the merchant princes nicknamed "the tribes" by the Cromwellians. Their names were Athy, Blake, Bodkin, Browne, D'Arcy, Deane, Ffont, Ffrench, Joyce, Kirwan, Lynch, Martin, Morris, Skerrett.

These families were very exclusive and closed the city to the native Irish, ordering that "neither O nor Mac shall strutte ne swagger thro the streets of Galway." That this did not sit well with the Irish tribes is attested to by the inscription which was once to be seen over the west gate: "From the fury of the O'Flahertys, good lord deliver us."

Now, not only do the O's and the Macs freely walk the streets, but the town is packed with tourists bearing names from every part of the globe.

Perhaps it is echoes of this early defensiveness, or perhaps the town is in retreat from the continuous attack of brigades of tourists—whatever the reason, for me there is something cool about this city, something shuttered in spite of the jumble of ancient, winding streets and the generous openness of the town square.

This city center, Eyre Square, with its kelly-green lawns and bright flower beds dedicated to John F. Kennedy, is an interesting place to be on a sunny day. My young daughter Erika discovered this fact on our arrival in Galway dazed after a week of travel and late-night talk.

It was noon. The benches were full, the green was dotted with reclining figures of office workers, students, and travelers, eating, sleeping, and playing guitars. My daughter rested, pillowing her head on a convenient incline in the greensward. There I left her with a bag of candy and ripe tomatoes while I explored the pubs that had been recommended to me on our journey.

On my return I found her chatting animatedly with a friendly young man. "Mom," she said, wide-eyed, "two tinker children woke me up. They wanted money and went up to every person saying, 'Pence, pence.' They were so raggedy, and the little girl was only about *five* years old. I gave them tomatoes, but they only wanted pence."

She was impressed, too, with Albert Powers's very touching and alive statue of Padraig O'Conaire, the great Gaelic writer. The statue, almost elfin, is seated on ivy-covered stones on an old Irish farm wall. His hat sits well back on his head, his eyes are downcast, his face contemplative, as though listening to some inner voice. Perhaps he is hearing the musical Gaelic of one of his own stories.

At one time O'Conaire was a member of the British Civil Service, but he gave that up and took to the road with a donkey and cart, which he thought was a better living. The poet F. R. Higgins wrote this elegy for Padraig, who was a close friend:

> They'll miss his heavy stick and stride in Wicklow—
> His story-talking down winetavern street,
> Where old men sitting in the wizened daylight
> Have kept an edge upon his gentle wit;
> While women of the grassy streets of Galway,
> Who hearken for his passing—but in vain,
> Shall hardly tell his step as shadows vanish
> Through archways of forgotten Spain.

It is the city of Galway that gave the expression "lynch law" to the English language. Oddly, time has reversed its meaning, although the original incident is still remembered.

By 1493, when James Lynch was elected Lord Mayor of Galway, the city already had an extensive history of trade and friendship with Spain. Wishing to strengthen these ties, the Lord Mayor took into his home as a sort of exchange student the young son of an influential Spanish merchant named Gomez. Young Gomez and the Lord Mayor's son Walter became great friends, until the Spaniard began paying frequent calls at the home of Walter's girlfriend Agnes. The reason, according to young Gomez, was that he enjoyed visiting because her father spoke fluent Spanish, but Walter thought the daughter rather than the father was the attraction.

One tragic day Walter's jealousy overcame his reason, and at the height of a furious argument he stabbed his friend to death. He was caught and brought to trial before the magistrate—his own father— who found him guilty and sentenced him to death.

On the day of execution father and son took the last sacrament together and went to the execution spot. A threatening mob had gathered, among them kinsmen of the culprit's mother, who were openly hostile to the carrying out of the sentence. The executioner dared not execute the boy—so the father, like Abraham, himself sacrificed his son to the principle of justice. But God did not reach out to stay his hand, and he went home a broken man, never to set foot outside his door again.

On Shop Street is Lynch's Castle, a fine old house built in 1320, the residence of the tragic family.

Near the Fish Market is the Spanish Arch, built in 1584 as an extension to the city wall in order to protect the quays. It now houses the Galway Museum. It probably received its name because it leads to the Spanish Parade, once a favorite promenade for the Spanish merchants and their families.

If you're in town some time around August 17, you'll be off to the races. Ask any old-timer about the Galway races and you'll get a knowing wink. "Ah, they'll be lying in the fields and everywhere that week," said one old gent to me. "Well," he sighed, "but it's not what it used to be."

The salmon both smoked and in its natural state is of course the king of
Irish fish and in demand everywhere. Due to overfishing the salmon's
future is, alas, precarious, unless urgent action is taken by the Government to curb overeager fishermen who are depleting the stocks by catching and selling immature fish. A recent development may however
divert some attention away from the costly salmon, and that is the
growth in popularity of smoked rainbow trout.

"Inside Ireland"

From what I hear, it's still a great auld celebration, with oceans of
Guinness and much laughter and music. As for what it used to be . . . I
can't imagine what they could possibly have done in the old days that
beats lying in the fields.

The city of Galway is wedged between the sea and the great expanse
of Lough Corrib, which stretches deep into the land of the west, covering sixty-eight square miles of the best fishing in the world. It is said to
have an island for every day of the year. These islands vary in size, from
verdant acres to tiny bird sanctuaries. One island is approached at your
own risk—it is patrolled by a mad one-horned goat.

At Galway the lough empties into the river Corrib and out to sea
into Galway Bay. Stand on the Weir Bridge spanning the river and
look down. If you're there in December, January, or February, you'll see
the annual miracle of thousands of salmon lying on the bed of the river.
They are waiting there for the rain to raise the water level so they can
leap up to their spawning grounds in the lakes and rivers.

THE GALLOWS
Eyre Square
Food: Lunch menu
There is a seventeenth-century gallows standing outside this pub, from
which it derives its macabre name. Inside is a cheerfully renovated saloon with a wooden ceiling and a large hexagonal bar, which sports a
gibbet and a noose, part of the relic outside. The atmosphere and fur-

nishings are clearly reminiscent of the old days; wainscotting, comfortable chairs and tables, photos of ships and Irish life in the Galway area.

Though The Gallows caters to the young business crowd, the ubiquitous old men in caps are also to be seen. There is a restaurant in the adjoining room that serves quite good food.

Though a pleasant place, it does seem tame to a man like Ben Kiely, who remembers:

> This pub in Eyre Square as I first remember it was a place where you might easily lose an eye if you were a tall man and happened to brush against the peaked tweed cap of one of the customers: caps that bristled with or were festooned with salmon lures and artificial flies. The one thing that made you feel happy was that the fish were reasonably safe while those fellows kept their caps on their heads. The female customers were not so adorned. Germaine Greer had not been heard of.
>
> As far as I remember there was even sawdust on the floor in those days . . . but now the sawmills, like the woods of Kilcash, are down and the floors are freshly hoovered and the fishermen have no panache—that is, if there are any of them in the place at all.

LARRY CULLEN'S
Foster Street

If you are confident without being insensitive and you want to be part of the earthier side of Irish pub life, Cullen's is definitely your spot.

It was recommended to me by a young Irish writer as being an "in" kind of place. Dark, dingy, and bearing the historical dirt of a few centuries, atmosphere is created by a few posters advertising Irish Traditional Music Festivals and some candles guttering in bottles. The communicants are young intellectuals, hip tourists, and regular workingmen.

I found myself in an immediate argument with a wild-looking Irishman with a front tooth missing. He was angry that I was writing a book about Ireland. "Why don't you write a guide to Irish toilets?" he asked rudely. "You could describe how full of Irish charm they are and make a few American dollars off our culture."

I decided to wade in and verbally slug it out with him. All the occupants of the bar soon chose sides and were cheering us on. Many pints later I decided to leave. A long-haired German student asked if he could photograph the two of us together. My erstwhile enemy flashed a wry grin of considerable if gap-toothed charm and we all went outside for a photographic session. The German, who, it turned out, was a friend of his, posed us with our arms companionably around each other's waist.

Suddenly aware of the ludicrous side of life, we were caught by the camera in a fit of laughter; now that photo represents a few Irish hours in a German travel diary.

For me the experience was a relief; the Irish usually mask their resentments behind the sly remark and the subtle needle; this straightforward approach, though somewhat heavy going, was cathartic for us all.

From Galway city, follow the wise salmon's example and make your way to the land so beautifully perceived by V. S. Pritchett:

> My mind fed on the scenery. The sight of lakes, slatey in the rain, or like blue eyes looking out of the earth in the changing Irish light; the Atlantic wind always silvering the leaves of beech and oak and elm on the road to Galway, empty except for a turf cart or a long funeral; the Twelve Pins in Connemara now gleaming like glass in the drizzle, now bald, green and dazzling; the long sea inlets that on hot days burn their way deeply inland beyond Clifden where the sands are white and the kelp burns on them.
>
> I do not think only of landscape but of the wide disheartening streets of the long villages and the ruined farms of the west; and the elaborately disguised curiosity of the impulsively kind but guarded people, looking into your eyes for a chance of capping your fantasy with one of theirs, in long ceremonies of well-mannered evasion, craving for the guesswork of acquaintance and diversion.

MAAM

BRIDGE BAR

Stop at Maam for refreshment beside the little bridge that fords the river. Joe Kerne, who runs this nice little pub next to the petrol pump and grocery store known as Maam, tells me his pub was built in 1840 by the same Scottish engineer who built the bridge.

The interior is whitewash-clean, with dark beams, a bay window, and a beautiful nineteenth-century bar. Doorways are pleasingly arched, and there is a dart room for those whose aim is true. You might be lucky and arrive when there is music; one never knows when the musicians will show up.

Your companions at the bar will be fishermen, travelers, and shepherds, and for the first time you may even hear Gaelic spoken unselfconsciously.

There are more sheep in Connemara than people; you'll see them feeding in the fields and along the roadside, bearing their shaggy gray coats on their spindly black legs. Sometimes farmers daub them with pale-pink or blue dye to distinguish the flocks, and you may find yourself slowly cruising behind a trotting flock of living pastel wool.

Route N59, the road to Clifden, winds through mile after beautiful mile of lakes, heather, streams, and bogland dotted with pools reflecting the sky. Farmers ride along the narrow roads on old bicycles, dressed in worn brown coats and muddy Wellingtons. They greet you with a wave or nod as you pass, as everyone does on Irish roads. In some rural areas a nod can look like a negative shake of the head, but don't be fooled, it is a *friendly* greeting.

Ahead loom the famous brotherhood of mountains called the Twelve Bens (or Pins), and to the right are the blue peaks of the Maamturks.

CLIFDEN

The main town of Connemara, Clifden is a good center from which to explore the area. Connemara seems to swallow people: no matter how many tourists flock there, the solitude is vast and healing. From Clifden you can strike out on a variety of inland or coastal rambles and return rejuvenated.

The town is two broad streets with brightly painted shops and a marketplace that in August is the site of the Connemara Pony Fair, honoring this hardy Irish horse. Breeders and enthusiasts arrive from all over the world to rub shoulders with the locals, the tinkers, and the three-card tricksters.

The Connemara pony is beloved for its diverse abilities as a work horse, hunter, jumper, race horse, and riding horse. A living result of Irish history, the first version of the pony arrived on Irish shores with the Celts, who brought with them steeds with a heritage tracing back to the original wild horse of the Ice Age (20,000 years ago). Andalusian horses mingled with these native herds when a part of the Spanish Armada was wrecked off the Galway coast. In the early nineteenth century yet another strain was introduced when the Irish began importing Arabians; the final result is today's plucky Connemara pony.

There are two excellent shops in Clifden: Millars, which produces handwoven tweeds in glowing colors and is a marvelous example of a local industry using local raw materials and labor to produce goods that are exported worldwide; and Stanley's—a real country store with a jumble of everything you could imagine, from fishing rods to high fashion to mattress ticking. There are also craft shops stocking the famous Connemara marble (visit the quarry at nearby Streamstown), Galway crystal, and tweeds.

KINGS BAR

Specialty: Seafood

A regular Irish pub with a special twist; excellent seafood suppers till 11:00 p.m.

If you want to catch your own, you can join the Clifden Anglers' Club (information at Stanley's Shop), which entitles you, for a very modest sum, to fish any of the small lakes on which the club maintains a boat (mainly brown trout): or you can obtain a license from the local garda (police) to fish for salmon and sea trout. For sea fishing, see John Ryan next to Ryan's Hardware.

The Connemara Golf Course, about ten miles south of Clifden, is so beautifully situated it's hard to keep your eye on the ball; stretches of fine, sandy beaches run beside it, and the Twelve Bens supervise your game from the distance (Ben means mountain).

The bane of the small-town publican's life is the loudmouthed loquacious customer who, keeping his drink in front of him for hours on end, warrants his presence in the bar by sips taken at fifteen minute intervals. The publican's admonition to such may well be the brutal but effective "Come on, pelt it down ye!" but I admire the approach of the spruce old widow, who, gazing over the rim of her glasses, rebuked the vehement with "Gentlemen, I'm afraid your conversation is curtailing your capacity."

—Danny Costello
"The Small-Town Pub"

ROUNDSTONE

If you follow the coast road from Clifden for the fourteen miles to Roundstone, you'll pass the monument to Alcock and Brown, whose pioneering trans-Atlantic flight in 1919 came to rest on a rocky hill near the town of Ballinaboy.

To enter Roundstone is to take a time-machine trip back to the nineteenth century. Beside the main road, facing the sea, is a curving row of Victorian houses, shops, pubs, and small cottages. Just north of the town at Gorteen Bay is a two-mile stretch of pure sand beach flanked by gentle dunes at one end and rock pools at the other.

CONNOLLY'S

Roundstone is a hideaway for a number of international artists and writers who come to Ireland, not only for the inspiration, but for the tax laws, which exempt writers and artists in residence.

Connolly's a cozy seaside pub, is the place where you will find them resting from their labors.

CLARINBRIDGE

PADDY BURKE'S OYSTER INN

Food: Excellent, with seafood a specialty

Paddy Burke's is one of Ireland's most renowned pubs and restaurants. It is a snug thatched pub genuinely traditional in atmosphere. The low ceiling is beamed, and there are high-backed benches and rope-seat stools. Small leaded windowpanes let in a soft light, and a large fieldstone fireplace reminds you of Ireland's reputation for hospitality. On the wall is an unusual painting of Blind Raftery the poet. His smile is oddly insinuating, in disconcerting contrast to his vacant eyes.

Raftery was a famous Irish-speaking bard who wandered this area in the eighteenth and early-nineteenth centuries. In keeping with the bardic tradition, his poetry was not written down but was memorized by generations of country folk. In his travels Raftery met and eulogized an outstanding local beauty named Mary Hynes. Apparently her reputation for beauty outlived Mary herself. People were still talking of her in

Yeats's day, with a local pride tinged with respectful fear, for such beauty was thought to have a bit of the "fairy" about it.

Raftery's poem to Mary was light and playful, but to Yeats's darker vision the poet and the girl were "perfect symbols of the sorrow of beauty and the magnificence and penury of dreams."

At the impeccably polished three-sided bar local people, visiting Dubliners, and tourists congregate. "Cars park themselves here automatically, you know," a Dublin man told me; "they're that used to making the stop. This area is called the Bermuda Triangle," he went on. "Between Paddy Burke's, Moran's the Weir, and the Kilkeene Graveyard, people have been known to completely disappear."

Clarinbridge is an oyster town, and in season (September–April) Paddy's serves these mouth-watering morsels fresh. They also feature a splendid variety of buffet foods to satisfy the most gourmet palate, and a Cordon Bleu menu at night (prices are fairly reasonable).

With all these delights, it is no wonder that this pub, in operation since 1835, should have been discovered and frequented by the famous and infamous. Royalty, both British and the Hollywood type, have made Paddy's a favorite port of call in Ireland, as have men and women prominent in international news.

Raftery the Poet

I am Raftery the poet
Full of hope and love,
With eyes without light
And calm without torment.

Going west on my journey
By the light of my heart,
Weak and tired
To my road's end.

Look at me now,
My face to the wall,
Playing music
To empty pockets.
                    —Anthony Raftery
                    (translated from the Irish by Frank O'Connor)

THE WEIR. KILCOLGAN

MORAN'S OYSTER COTTAGE,
also known as MORAN'S THE WEIR

Food: Outstanding smoked salmon, oysters, and seafood salad

Turn off route N18 as indicated by the small signs advertising Moran's (about twelve miles out of the city of Galway, just south of Clarinbridge) for a real treat.

Moran's (pronounced *More*-ans) is a 200-year-old thatched cottage right beside the waters of the Kilcolgan River.

Quite simply, the oysters and salmon you eat here are the best you will ever have—anywhere. Add a few slices of homemade brown bread baked by Mrs. Moran, and a pint of swarthy, creamy-headed Guinness from the tap, and you've a meal to remember.

The place is run by young Willie Moran, the seventh generation to own the oyster beds that are situated at the mouth of the Kilcolgan River, part of the 700 acres of sea that form the Galway Bay oysterbed. Willie is a cheery host with an easy friendliness and open enthusiasm about his work.

"Hookers used to stop here on their way from Connemara," he told me as we delved into Moran's history.

Hookers? I was astonished at the vision of this healthy country spot as a way station for Connemara girls-gone-wrong.

To my relief, he went on to explain that hookers were actually heavy sailing ships built to transport turf. I also learned that during the famine the weir, or stone wall, was constructed across the river to trap the salmon, giving Moran's its name.

Willie showed me around the old Moran homestead, now "Moran's." It was still recognizably a cottage, with its small bar and wood-burning stove where once the kitchen was, and a cozy little snug that had, appropriately, served generations of Morans as a bedroom. A dining room has been added with a pass-through bar and kitchen counter. The walls are pristine white, the floor brown tile. On the walls are many amusing photos of world luminaries who have come to this simple place. A friend tells me he once met the then-President of Ireland, Charles Haughey, over a plate of salmon at Moran's, which shows, my friend says, expertise and sound judgment on Haughey's part.

Though 140 sides of smoked salmon and 1,000 oysters are consumed daily at the height of the season, the place always seems relaxed and congenial. In the summer, you can take your pint and sit out on the terrace watching the punters and fishermen at work and perhaps have a plate of Mrs. Moran's celestial salmon salad.

If you're having oysters, you can be assured that it's only been an hour since they were raked into baskets and minutes since they were opened. Willie is a champion oyster shucker. At the annual Oyster Festival (September 14, 15, 16) in Clarinbridge, he opened thirty oysters in one minute and thirty seconds.

This is not the only startling statistic involving Moran's: a certain Hugh Williams once devoured 158 of Galway's best in an hour and fifty minutes. Understandably perhaps, his name is illegible in the guest book.

With the advent of popularity, the Morans, displaced from their cottage, moved into a modern, somewhat soulless, brick abode nearby. To an outsider, the move might seem sad, but the Morans were perfectly happy to exchange character for convenience.

This is a trend all over the west. Irish country folk are moving from their "quaint" whitewashed cabins with no plumbing or heating to ugly but sturdy brick buildings with TV antennas and wall-to-wall carpeting. Many of the lovely thatched cottages you see belong now to foreigners who have bought and restored them, enamored of their simple beauty and elemental character.

GORT

Still traveling south from Galway on N18, you reach Gort, once the dwelling place of Guaire, King of Connaught in the seventh century (page 164). The land around Gort is stitched with streams that run in and out of the rock. One such place of watery hide-and-seek is called Raftery's Cellars, after the poet.

To the north of the town is Coole Park, formerly the residence of Lady Gregory, one of the founders of the Abbey Theatre and author of the famous one-act play *The Rising of the Moon*. Coole Park was the rendezvous for renowned poets, writers, and artists of that turbulent and creative era from 1904 to 1916. It is now a national forest, and on a tree known as the Autograph Tree you will find initials carved by Lady Gregory's celebrated visitors: George Bernard Shaw, Sean O'Casey, Augustus John, Oliver St. John Gogarty, John Masefield, and Douglas Hyde, the first President of Ireland.

Stroll through Coole Park and you will surely understand how its peaceful woods and lakes influenced Yeats and inspired his work: "And yet the woods at Coole . . . are so much more knitted to my thoughts that when I am dead they will have, I am persuaded, my longest visit," he wrote.

Lady Augusta Gregory, who made Coole Park a center for the Irish literary revival, was the truest friend Yeats ever had. She was the widow of Sir William Gregory, an urbane member of the land-owning class in Galway, and when Yeats met her she was forty-five years old. Yeats gave a verbal snapshot of her at that time, describing her as "without obvious good looks except the charm that comes from strength, intelligence and kindness."

Four miles northeast of Gort (you'll see the signs) is Thoor Ballylee. Yeats bought the tower, a square, four-story Norman keep with adjacent cottages and gardens and restored it. In the early 1920s he summered there, and it became one of the most important symbols in the landscape of Irish literature.

Again and again the tower figures in the poetry of Yeats, transmuted by him into a multilayered symbol for sexual, mythic, magical, and historic forces, and finally into a symbol for his own person.

> *Blessed be this place,*
> *More blessed still this tower;*
> *A bloody, arrogant power*
> *Rose out of the race*
> *Uttering, mastering it,*
> *Rose like these walls from these*
> *Storm-beaten cottages—*
> *In mockery have I set*
> *A powerful emblem up,*
> *And sing it rhyme upon rhyme*
> *In mockery of a time*
> *Half dead at the top. . . .*

Is every modern nation like the tower,
Half dead at the top?

Thoor Ballylee is open to the public. When Yeats lived there, the walls were electric blue and the ceilings multicolored. They are now white, but otherwise the tower is much as he left it, with some of the heavy oak furniture that he had specially designed still on view.

A stone bearing an inscription by Yeats was placed on the front wall after his death:

I the poet William Yeats,
With old millboards and sea-green slates,
And smithy work from the Gort forge,
Restored this tower for my wife George;
And may these characters remain
When all is ruin once again.

THE LITTLE WONDER BAR

Picture an evening in August. The Irish twilight is taking its beautiful time bathing the countryside in mother-of-pearl (Ireland is in the northern latitudes and in the summer twilight lasts till 11:00 p.m.). A large moon is rising over the spacious town square of Gort, and music and singing from numerous pubs mingle in the quiet air.

It is the evening of the Rose of Gort Festival. Every other house on the square is a pub, and they are all full. The Little Wonder Bar is on the corner, and inside, the caeli band (a caeli is a country dance and get-together) is playing trance music to inspire the feet of the dancers, young and old.

Some festivals in Ireland are, understandably, the creations of Bord Failte (tourist board) as a means of bringing tourist money to needy areas, but this festival seemed to be truly local; few camera toters were in sight.

The dancers stepped and twirled, children dashed about, and old men sat in a side room drinking their pints and watching TV. *Kojak* reaches into even the most indigenous of celebrations.

SULLIVAN'S HOTEL

The other side of the square from The Little Wonder Bar is the taproom at Sullivan's.

Sullivan's is the place where the Rose of Gort contest is judged, and the lively crowd I saw was sprinkled with dressed-up young girls and boys; men in dark suits rushed around importantly.

In the bar, space had been cleared for step dancing, and two little girls were demonstrating their style, arms held straight at their sides, hair bouncing. Step dancing is popular in Ireland, and contests are held at a national level.

The band, as usual, were local men who played as a part of life instead of as a living. They played jigs and reels, hornpipes and sets, with great verve, pieces with names like "The Rocky Road to Dublin," "The Harvest Home," "Paddy Whack," "The Drop of Brandy," which joined them to their precursors in the eighteenth and nineteenth centuries who played these same tunes. In those earlier days, dancing had become so popular that it led to the creation of a vast body of music; a conservative estimate would exceed 4,000 individual pieces.

Standing beside me at Sullivan's was the only other foreigner in view, a young Frenchman. "So nice are these musicians here," he said, "one he even gaves me his bodhran to play and leaves me to sit into a set." He beamed at me, doubly delighted with his success at speaking English and playing Irish.

GEAHAN'S

Geahan's is the fashionable pub. There are old photos, wicker lampshades, an up-to-date jukebox, a pleasant back room, and a billiard table. The crowd consists of foreign students, local gentry, visiting intellectuals, and the usual complement of regular folk. Conversation is spirited and stimulating, and people include you more readily than is customary in the average Irish pub.

Geahan's also sponsors the Gort Poetry Contest, being well aware of the tower four miles away that keeps the memory of W. B. Yeats forever green and the students of poetry forever arriving.

COUNTY MAYO

Mayo, like all of Ireland, has been powerfully shaped by history, by the life of the past within the present, but its secret form does not reveal itself to the conventional techniques of research. It is locked within the voice, within song, legend, traditions wedded to place and within stones.

—Thomas Flanagan

LECANVEY

Lecanvey lies beside Clew Bay, a superb expanse of island-dotted sea framed by mountain ranges. Inland is a vastness of red bog broken by thin ribbons of road and dark-green lakes: Lough Mask, Lough Conn, Lough Carra.

Rearing up 2,510 feet beside the bay is the unmistakable cone shape of Croagh Patrick. Every year, on the last Sunday in July, the mountain's solitude is broken by a national pilgrimage when thousands of people, some barefoot, climb its flanks to hear Mass celebrated on the summit. Added to the satisfaction of having done one's religious duty is the reward of a spectacular view from Croagh Patrick's crown. Thackeray rhapsodized in his *Irish Sketch Book:*

> I caught sight not only of a fine view, but of the most beautiful view I ever saw in the world. . . . A miracle of beauty . . . the Bay, and the Reek, which sweeps down to the sea, and a hundred islands in it, were dressed up in gold and purple, and crimson, with the whole cloudy west in a flame.

Croagh Patrick is Ireland's "Holy Mountain," for it was here in 441 that the patron saint of the land spent the forty days of Lent in prayer for the people of Ireland.

Patrick was taken to Ireland as a slave and herded sheep among the misty hills until he managed to escape. Once home, however, he had a dream in which the people cried out to him, "We beg you, holy youth, come and work once more among us." In 432 he returned to Ireland to spread the Word.

He must have been a spellbinding speaker, for the Irish not only took to Christianity with unbridled enthusiasm but spread their new belief with great zeal to the four corners of the earth.

Though Patrick and his crosier triumphed over the old Druidic order, the pagan proclivity for procreation and nature did not die, but was merely submerged, to live on in the collective unconscious of the Irish people.

The Irish have themselves written and spoken streams of words on the subject of "guilt," and perhaps this self-conscious conflict is but the ongoing struggle between the Druids and St. Patrick for the Irish soul.

PEGGY STAUNTON'S

This typically shabby country pub with its low ceiling, small windows, and the usual clutter of gewgaws behind the bar is a truly friendly place.

There is, in any case, something heartwarming about coming inside from the immense loneliness of the Mayo skies. Peggy Staunton adds to this sense of comforting humanity with a bright, matter-of-fact humor. Customers are lively and easy to talk to. There is also a concrete billiard room off the bar, with low windows offering the mountains a peep at the goings-on of the humans inside.

I had a few games with the German hitchhikers I had picked up

---

WINTER IN THE WEST

A drunken man in winter leans more heavily on the bar. He often seeks to draw another drinker or two to his side. Such a group creates a tight circle of privacy around itself—a privacy physically expressed by the arms they lay across one another's shoulders. Then, with faces almost touching, they appear to join closely in evident despair. This despair is not expressed in discussion among the drinkers. Rather, they exchange silence as if it were words, and words in brief expressions of the lonesomeness.

—Hugh Brody
Inishkillane

(hitching in Ireland is easy, safe, and a practical way to make friends). They were a delightful pair, a father and his eleven-year-old daughter— Horst and Katrin.

As Katrin and I bashed the balls about, we became aware that more than the mountains were peering at us through the window. At the level of the sill were two pairs of round eyes and a couple of tousled towheads. Every time we glanced their way, they disappeared, ducking down below the sill. Finally, they dared all and came in to play with us. I'm sorry to say that the five-year-old almost had me beat.

WESTPORT

The city of Westport lies in a hollow surrounded by trees and groves just off the shores of Clew Bay. It is another Irish town with a river flowing through it. On both sides of the river a spacious mall is planted refreshingly with lime trees. The town is well known as a fishing center.

TOMMIE NOLAN'S
Hard by the benevolent town square, which is really an ellipse, is this charming pub with gardens where country people in for the day mix with the regulars from the town and nearby housing estates.

In a beautiful demesne one and a half miles from town is Westport House, home of the Marquess of Sligo. The Georgian house, with a nine-bayed façade and eagles at the cornices, is filled with silver, paintings, and crystal, and is open to the public April to September from 2:00 to 6:00 p.m. The grounds contain a zoo, and hidden in the woods is a church with an especially handsome interior.

Westport House "illustrates one of the mysteries of Irish economy," says the Irish writer James Plunkett, "that however impoverished the life of the ordinary people, there was always room for a lord."

For many years powerful Anglo-Irish landlords, particularly in the west and in Mayo, held the land in their grip. Planted in the country by Cromwell, they lived in alien Georgian, Palladian mansions and collected rent from the peasants who scratched out a living among the stones. When the people failed to pay, they were evicted and their cabins razed to make room for cattle.

The ruling families differed from the native population in language, in religion; in fact, even in the notion of what constitutes a culture. They could not conceive of the farmers and peasants as having the same mentality and emotions as themselves, thinking them rather a form of human closer in nature to animals.

But in time Ireland absorbed these families, too, as it did the Vikings and Normans before them, and now the halls of Westport House, like many a manor, echo only to the footsteps of tourists and those interested in history.

A landlord in Ireland can scarcely invent an order which a servant, labourer, or cottar dares to refuse to execute. Nothing satisfies him but an unlimited submission. Disrespect, or anything tending towards sauciness, he may punish with his cane or his horsewhip with the most perfect security; a poor man would have his bones broke if he offered to lift his hands in his own defense. Landlords of consequence have assured me that many of their cottars would think themselves honoured by having their wives and daughters sent for to the bed of their master; a mark of slavery that proves the oppression under which such people must live. . . .

It must strike the most careless traveller to see whole strings of carts whipped into a ditch by a gentleman's footman to make way for his carriage; if they be overturned or broken in pieces no matter, it is taken in patience; were they to complain they would perhaps be horsewhipped.

—Arthur Young (1741–1820)
A Landlord's Amusement

It was against such conditions that the people rose in rebellion for the first time in 1798.

Not that all the lords were without a kind of misguided compassion: when Ireland was decimated by the savage famine of the 1840s the west was particularly hard-hit. Over a million people died, starving to death among the blighted fields. Two million fled the country, many to die in the ships that were taking them to a new life.

In Mayo, hundreds of starving peasants knelt on the steps of Westport House, in supplication to Lord Sligo. He did what he could, but finally gave up, placing the blame for the horror around him on poor administration of the Soup Kitchen Act.

In our times we have witnessed on television the pitiful bodies and terrible vacant eyes of the starving of India. The famine of 1846–47 had its reporters, too:

A calm, still horror was over all the land. Go where you would, in the heart of the town or in the church, on the mountainside or on the level plain, there was the stillness and heavy pall-like feeling of the chamber of death. You stood in the presence of a dread, silent, vast dissolution. . . . Human passion there was none, but inhuman and unearthly quiet. Children met you, toiling heavily on stone heaps, but their burning eyes were senseless, and their faces cramped and weasened like stunted old men. Gangs worked, but without a murmur, or a whistle or a laugh, ghostly, like voiceless shadows to the eye. Even womanhood had ceased to be womanly. The birds of the air carolled no more, and the crow and the raven dropped dead upon the wing. The very dogs, hairless, with the hair down, and the vertebrae of the back protruding like the saw of a bone, glared at you from the ditchside with a wolfish avid eye, and then slunk away scowling and cowardly. Nay, the sky of heaven, the blue mountains, the still lake stretching far away westward, looked not as their wont. Between them and you rose up a steaming agony, a film of suffering, impervious and dim.

—John Mitchell

The fateful years of the famine marked the beginning of a tragic diaspora for Ireland, when the main export of the country became her young people. Now the exodus has stopped and the prosperity that has arrived with membership in the European Economic Community assures a measure of stability, even with the inevitable economic slumps and the doldrums of long and draining strikes.

Lured by strong tax incentives, foreign industry has arrived, pumping new life into towns like Galway and Killala in the west. Today, overseas investment in Irish plants totals $4 billion, and foreign firms now employ one-third of Ireland's manufacturing labor force.

Farming, too, was revolutionized by membership in the Common Market. In six years farm income jumped from $710 million to $1.5 billion. So quick was the leap into prosperity that many farmers have not adjusted their life style, still riding in battered old cars, called bangers, and living as they have always lived in the Irish countryside.

To some, however, the changes wrought in Irish life by the economic boom do not seem totally beneficial:

> We had for a long time a stagnant economy, a rural society with no expectation of anything better, and most people were curiously content with their lot. Those who weren't content left, so we exported our tensions. This has changed. The tensions are here, expressed in a new materialism. Our society has become notably more selfish, highly competitive, everybody looking out for themselves. They want to take our increased wealth in terms of higher incomes now, rather than to plough it back into savings and investments for the future.
>
> —Garret FitzGerald,
> Leader of the *Fine Gael* party

There is concern about the industrialization of Ireland, as foreign smokestacks become part of the Irish landscape. German and Dutch vacation homes dot the land and cause a reaction only superficially humorous when they are referred to by the Irish as the new invaders of Ireland.

There is, however, no really serious threat. Ireland will incorporate these newcomers just as she has always done.

CASTLEBAR

Castlebar is the county seat of Mayo. Its crowded city center, with its shopfronts grafted onto eighteenth- and nineteenth-century buildings, is none too attractive, but walk down Castle Street to the tree-lined mall, a wide, spacious square of well-tended grass presided over by a handsome courthouse, and you'll sense the town as it once was. Looking around at the monuments, you will gain a feeling for the very special place that Castlebar holds in Irish history, for here was won a major battle in the rebellion of 1798, "the year of the French."

This insurrection is often called "the rebellion of the younger sons," because so many of its leaders came from prominent Anglo-Irish and even noble families. Inspired by the French Revolution and disgusted at the tyranny of their own class, these high-born young men ignited the people to revolt. Their ultimate objective was an Irish Republic, and though they failed, they were the first harbingers of what was to come.

It was to help the Irish rebels that three French frigates dropped anchor in Killala Bay one August morning in 1798. They brought with them 5,000 firelocks with which to arm the locals, 1,100 French troops, and a commander, General Joseph Humbert.

After they landed, an ill-sorted army began to form, made up of French regulars, hardened mercenaries, and a motley multitude of Gaelic-speaking peasants equipped with unfamiliar weapons and pikes hammered out on country forges.

This ragtag and dedicated army picked up momentum and hundreds of recruits at every crossroad as they marched through the land. In a famous nighttime maneuver, General Humbert and his men, their way lit by the straw torches of the populace, crept up on the town of Ballina and won it from the militia. Again moving by night, they marched on to Castlebar, where in a dawn raid they smashed and routed the forces of the crown.

A president of the Republic of Connaught was chosen, and while the leaders of the uprising were mostly farmers and peasants, the man who received this honor was not. He was John Moore, and came not from a humble cabin, but from the great Mayo estate of Moore Hall at Lough Carra.

The French general and his amazing army moved victoriously through several Mayo towns, fighting their way from the grassy slopes outside Castlebar into Sligo and Leitrim, strange land to many of the Mayo farm boys forming the core of the rebel army. The end came in Ballinamuck, where vastly superior British troops trapped the insurgents in a bog and annihilated them. The men of Mayo and their French comrades were defeated, but the dream of a free Ireland had been born and would not die.

The French and the Irish that were with them came on the mountain road from Crossmolina. They had little light cannon they dragged with them. 'Twas midnight when they got here to Lahardane, and they stopped for an hour at the Fair Green beyond. They came to free Ireland, but a lot of people at the time were afraid and didn't rightly understand. The people gathered about them in the Green but they couldn't understand the French language. The French were going by another road, but Father Conroy, the parish priest, told them to take the way by the Windy Gap.

They took it and they drove in all the cattle about the Gap. They went on then to Castlebar and they won a big battle there. The Irish fought well with them there, but they'd fight better if they were trained. . . .

There was a man from this neighborhood, Larry Gillespie, that followed Humbert too. He was in the fighting at Ballinamuck . . . but he was arrested and taken in to Ballina. After being tried, he was sentenced to be hanged. He was only a short time married and his wife went to the jail. She took a bottle of poteen with her that she gave to the guards, and they let her in to see him. The two of them exchanged clothes and Larry got out. He raced for Ennis and was never taken. Next morning Larry was missed, and they brought the wife before the same judges that ordered Larry to be hanged. "Well," says Lord Portarlington, "since Larry can't be hanged now, there's nothing for it but to give a reprieve to his wife." Larry got away to France and stayed there seventeen years, and when he came back he found his wife married.

—recorded by Richard Hayes
The Last Invasion of Ireland

THE HUMBERT INN

A pub is the poor man's university.
—Sign in The Humbert Inn

This is the very inn that served as headquarters for the French forces in 1798. It is appropriately dark, a little musty, and packed with interesting memorabilia, not all of it from the days of the rebellion. There are two bottle corkers from 1900, whips and cudgels from an English jail in the Castlebar of the early nineteenth century, nineteenth-century panniers, and other objects of this ilk.

All is not strictly historical here, though; there is a back room for pool enthusiasts.

KILLALA

Here follow two Mayo pubs—both in Killala—visited and commented upon by the writer Thomas Flanagan, whose book *The Year of the French* gives a riveting account of events and personalities of 1798. He is presently at work on a second novel, this one set in nineteenth-century Ireland.

THE KERRYMAN
Kilcummin Road

To the left of the door to The Kerryman is a large stone set in a bed of earth and grass. This is said to be the stone General Humbert stepped on when he landed. It was moved here from the strand at Kilcummin, no mean feat considering its weight and size and the fact that it was moved by cart. Propped up against a stile behind the rock is a fading painting of what was once the sign for The Kerryman in the days when it was called The General Humbert. It shows a windswept cove with three French ships at anchor and a heroic Humbert standing on the shore waving his hat in one hand and the tricolor in the other.

"In the pub," writes Flanagan, "I had a whiskey with the local schoolmaster and a friend of mine, a bookseller from Ballina. At the far end of the bar, three small-farmers stood before their pints of Guinness, avoiding our conversation with the careful, instinctive courtesy of Mayo. For a 30-acre farmer, a round of pints with a friend is a serious social and financial occasion. . . .

" 'You will still find a few of the old families here and there,' the schoolmaster said, 'but most of them are gone.' His voice was soft, neutral. In the pubs of rural Ireland, matters of any delicacy are discussed in low tones; it is a bad country for the hard of hearing."

THE CRUISKEEN LAWN (THE LITTLE FULL JUG)

The weather had broken and a fine mist of rain drifted against the windows, but inside The Cruiskeen Lawn we were held safe and dry by the blanket of Irish conversation. . . . We were all trying to imagine ourselves into the passions and motives of those peasant soldiers who had marched upon Killala, of those thousands of rebels who had joined the army after the capture of Ballina and the great victory at Castlebar. They had not been moved, surely, by the abstract nationalism expressed in ballads composed for the centenary . . . and in the centenary statues of pike-clutching patriots.

But we were separated from them by a river of time bridged only by half-forgotten legends, stories handed down within families.

Though Thomas Flanagan wrote of his congenial experience in *this* pub, if you take pub-luck in this little town of 4,000, you will hear in practically all of them stories and songs about the history of Mayo.

BALLYHAUNIS

Here's another Mayo pub with the imprimatur of a writer, in this case the famous Irish playwright Hugh Leonard.

Aside from being an impressive literary man, Mr. Leonard is also a connoisseur of the public house in Ireland. "I have had the great good fortune to be a judge in the finals of the 'Top Pub' contest for three years which really provided the groundwork for a well-earned Ph.D. Pub-Hunting Diploma," he remarks. His choice and comment:

VAL'S BAR

"Halfway up a muddy main street, this is an oasis in the desert of east Mayo. The bar is small, warm, bright and welcoming; there is usually a turf fire burning, and the pub grub is excellent. I have traveled miles out of my way across the flat, wet bogland, just to call at Val's and bask in the friendliness."

PONTOON

HEALY'S ANGLERS' HOTEL

Healy's is six yards away from the waters of Lough Conn. I didn't measure the distance myself, but was so informed by Tom Healy, the friendly proprietor.

There is an inspirational view of the lough from three wide windows, and over the bar you can see a former denizen of its waters, a 28-pound pike caught by a proud angler in 1899.

Also adding their own special flavor are a stuffed pine martin and two wild geese standing guard in the hallway.

There is something wonderfully off-beat and relaxing about Healy's, and there's just a hint of mystery, too.

COUNTY SLIGO

I know we were both very close to tears and remember with wonder—for I
have never known anyone that cared for such mementoes—that I longed
for a sod of earth from some field I knew, something of Sligo to hold in my
hand.

—W. B. Yeats
Autobiographies

SLIGO

Sligo, a thriving merchants' metropolis, is northwest Ireland's most important town. It sits mostly on the south side of the river Garavogue
and is encircled on three sides by mountains. That is Sligo's physical
position; it is also at the center of "Yeats Country."

Though Yeats was born in Dublin, he spent so much of his childhood
in Sligo County that it became his adopted home. His stern sea captain
grandfather, William Pollexfen, made his home in the town of Sligo,
and on Wine Street you can still see the turret from which he swept the
harbor with a telescope, checking on his ships.

Young Yeats formed his imagination around the strong impressions
he received here: the beaches and mountains rich with legends; the stories told to him by country folk; the eccentricities of his varied relations—Uncle George the astrologer, who weighed his clothes before
donning them; Henry Middleton, a recluse who locked his door to the
world; the old servant Mary Battle, who was a clairvoyant. From these
ingredients, the poet wove a thick web of personal and mystic imagery,
an intensely Irish mythology.

Though Yeats died in 1939, he is still very much alive in Sligo. The
Yeats International Summer School, held each August, is organized to
service a wide range of students. There are lectures and field trips, plays
and films. In the evening drinking hours the school carries on the tradition of Gaelic courts of poetry: any participant will find an audience full
of goodwill and encouragement to spur him on in verse or song. (For
details, write to the Yeats Society, Sligo, County Sligo.)

The County Library and Museum has, in addition to its valuable collection of letters, photographs, and first editions of W. B. Yeats's poems, an impressive collection of paintings by his well-known brother, Jack Butler Yeats.

It is not surprising that Sligo has a fine bookshop: Keohanes in Castle Street is a treasure trove of Irish literature. After browsing here, why not go to Hardagan's for a pint or two.

HARDAGAN'S
Old Market Street

Formerly the domain of men, Hardagan's now permits females to enjoy its time-burnished recesses. There is a big old marble bar and an impressive wall of antique, slightly warped condiment drawers supported by carved wooden arches.

Four snugs house the laughter and chat of the locals. Each snug has a special feature of its own: one has little glass doors on hinges that open to the barman behind the bar, another has a door giving direct access to the bar, the third has a private entry door from the street, and the fourth is extremely tiny. The whole arrangement smacks of the cozy comforts of an old-fashioned railway carriage conducive to long bouts of drink and talk; based on the sounds I heard from my seat at the bar, the inhabitants were indeed embarked on a journey of a kind.

McLYNN'S
Old Market Street

The crowded back room at McLynn's offers a potpourri of people, from fierce young students to dedicated members of the Sinn Fein to prosperous professional men. There is music and singing here of both the spontaneous and rehearsed varieties.

Loud, gregarious, and fun.

BEEZIE'S
O'Connell Street

This hostelry is dedicated to the memory of Beezie Gallagher in reverence and respect for a truly remarkable woman.

Beezie was born in the 1860's and reared on Cottage Island in Lough

Gill near Sligo town. Her early years were spent as a house-maid to the Wynne family, who at that time lived in Hazelwood House; the demesne of which spread out on all sides to include Lough Gill and surrounding countryside.

She later returned to spend all of her adult life on the island she loved. It was there she developed the many fascinating characteristics which make her remembered today.

Being so alone and protected from society, she turned to nature for her companionship. The birds, squirrels, domestic animals and even the rodents grew to trust and love her. Jimbo McCarrick, her great friend and protector, tells of the swans sitting in her kitchen and eating from her hand, and again of her banning from the island a visitor who dared to throw a stone at a friendly rat.

Her knowledge and love of the lake was unsurpassed. Following the Great Blizzard of 1947, she returned by row-boat alone after one brief week of recuperation, having been removed from the island suffering from malnutrition—the confinement of the County Home being quite unbearable for her although she was in her early 80's.

The most endearing aspect of her personality was her natural sense of hospitality and welcome, and it is this we would most like to emulate here in O'Connell St., Sligo. The many and frequent visitors to Lough Gill would be always welcome to call, and the kettle would be boiled or the damp coat dried with the natural graciousness of the true hostess. She might then recount the famous visitors to Hazelwood House in her youth and imitate in a most talented fashion their speech and movement. Whatever the story or the circumstances of the visit the time spent with Beezie was always entertaining and the impact of her noble character guaranteed she was never forgotten.

Beezie died on the island she loved in 1951. She had visited Sligo town on Christmas Eve and had rowed out to her home from Dooney Rock nearby. When friends came to cut timber for her some days later, they found her burned to death in her island home.

With her passed another age, another time, when life was slower, nature closer and hospitality normal.

—Brochure for visitors to Beezie's

Dedicated to one of Sligo's loveliest spirits, Beezie's is spacious and tasteful. From the moment the traveler steps under the green awning and enters the pleasingly Victorian ambience of palm trees, stained glass, and lamps with green glass shades, he is sure of respite from weariness.

The long front bar is partitioned in classic Irish style. The central lounge is peacefully illuminated by a large skylight, and a marble-columned fireplace with green tile adds a nice touch.

On the wall, among other things, are photos of Beezie, which make you wish you knew her, and an amusing extract from an Irish travel diary dated 1877.

The rushing Garavogue River, which flows two and a half miles directly into Lough Gill, gives Sligo its particular flavor. Ben Kiely remembers:

> Jack B. Yeats once, half in fun, told a friend of mine that he had learned to paint by leaning over (he may have said spitting over) the Garavogue bridge; the second bridge that is, in the centre of Sligo town and the last before the water turns salt: the bridge that has the cataract and the music of falling water to mock the grunts and belches of the traffic. When the river is at the top of its form it's quite easy to see what the painter meant. The smooth black water turns the corner, holds its breath for a while and hesitates when it realizes what's in store for it, then takes the plunge; breaking up into all shapes and patterns and colors, revealing in a moment all the beauty it had stored up during its long reverie two miles upstream in Lough Gill.

Lough Gill is full of islands, the most prominent of which is the beautifully wooded Cottage Island, where Beezie lived and where, among the trees, you can find the ruins of an ancient church. On the south shore, near Cottage Island, is Dooney Rock, celebrated by Yeats in "The Fiddler of Dooney."

I drove on the road to the southeastern end of Lough Gill with my two German friends still in the car. We stopped so an entranced Katrin could feed the famous swans the remains of our lunch bread. She called to them in German, and being international, they glided to us with a wonderful, bath-toy weightlessness that still managed to be regal.

The gentle mountains that look down on three sides of the lough are lush with vegetation, and there is a unique softness to the air. It's not

hard to understand how this romantic spot worked magic on the youthful heart of Yeats and filled the images of his early poetry:

The Lake Isle of Innisfree

I will arise and go now, and go to Innisfree,
And a small cabin build there, of clay and wattles made;
Nine bean rows will I have there, a hive for the honey bee,
　　And live alone in the bee-loud glade.

And I shall have some peace there, for peace comes dropping slow,
Dropping from the veils of the morning to where the cricket sings;
There midnight's all a-glimmer, and noon a purple glow,
　　And evening full of the linnet's wings.

I will arise and go now, for always night and day
I hear lake water lapping with low sounds by the shore;
While I stand on the roadway, or on the pavements gray,
　　I hear it in the deep heart's core.

Horst, Katrin, and I gazed from the shore at the tiny island made world-famous by the poet. It looked dreamy and wild enough to satisfy even me, a terminal romantic. We debated swimming out to it but settled for sitting on a rock in the sun. Katrin fished hopefully nearby, and Horst spoke to me of his war-bruised childhood in the bomb-hollowed shell of Berlin. A heron flapped by, and war and sorrow were far away and unreal.

North of Lough Gill is a pleasant region of small limestone hills and ferny glens. Four miles from the town of Sligo, near Fermoyle, is the immense, megalithic tomb of Leacht con Mhic Ruis (the Stone of Cu, Son of Ros). From the tomb which commands the top of a hill, there is a fine view of the Lough Gill area and of the coast.

ROSSES POINT

All of Rosses Point was once owned by Yeats's cousins the Middletons, whose early ancestors were smugglers there. They lived in a large mansion called Elsinore, which they believed to be haunted by a window-tapping spirit. The house stands facing the sea in the grasslands that slope down below Ryan's Hotel and, last I heard, was owned by the Bruens.

The Bruens hail from a family of old salts and run a properly wind-washed pub overlooking the harbor. I've not been there myself, so don't know if it still exists in these days of rapid change. From what I heard of their homemade apple tart, I hope it does.

Another pub recommended to me but not personally explored at Rosses Point is Austie's. So here at last is your chance to become your own pub guide without previous comments from me to distract your judgment—and I am momentarily free of responsibility.

When I look at my brother's picture *Memory Harbour*—houses and an-chored ships and distant lighthouse all set close together as in some old map—I recognize in the blue-coated man with the mass of white shirt the pilot I went fishing with, and I am full of disquiet and of excitement, and I am melancholy because I have not made more and better verses. I have walked on Sinbad's yellow shore and never shall another hit my fancy.

—W. B. Yeats
"Memory of Rosses Point"

DRUMCLIFFE

The magnificent twenty-two miles from Sligo to Bundoran are high above the bay of Drumcliffe, passing the access road to Drumcliffe churchyard, where W. B. Yeats lies buried. This road is marked, some-how appropriately, by an ancient Celtic cross and the remains of a round tower. Rooks gather in the old trees around the church, and in among the wild grasses and gravestones is a plain slab of limestone car-rying the message written by Yeats himself as his epitaph:

Cast a cold eye
On life, on death.
Horseman, pass by!

Of course, with lovely Irish irony, no one simply passes by. Horse-men and travelers using more modern means of transport linger and cast anything but a cold eye. Fortunately, however, there are no great tourist hordes or buses, just a few people wandering about in the peaceful shade. Sometimes an admirer will lay a fresh flower upon the grave, where it glows against the gravel covering.

Though Yeats died in Paris, he requested burial in Sligo, picking this particular churchyard because his great-grandfather had once been rector there.

Drumcliffe is flanked by the extraordinary, flat-topped landmark of Benbulben Mountain on one side and Knocknarea Mountain on the other. Knocknarea is traditionally considered to be the tomb of Maeve, the first century A.D. Queen of Connaught. On the summit is the great cairn within which it is said she lies, a mound of stones with a slope 80 feet high, a diameter 100 feet at the top and 630 feet around the bottom. A number of satellite tombs surround the cairn, keeping Maeve company in death. This warrior queen of the ancient sagas is another female personification of Ireland, another manifestation of the Irish fertility goddess.

Maeve is one of the central figures of the famous saga *Tain Bo Cuailgne* ("The Cattle Raid of Cooley"). This tale, part of the Ulster Cycle, is a kind of Irish *Iliad,* wild, stirring, and full of violent nobility, the oldest vernacular epic in Western literature.

Basically the story is about a power struggle. Maeve and her husband, Ailill, talking in bed one night, get around to comparing their riches: they are equal in all things except one—Ailill possesses a magnificent bull of divine origin. Maeve is not the kind of woman to take this news lying down.

She learns of another such bull on the Cooley Peninsula in Louth and immediately offers all manner of gifts to its owner, including her own "friendly thighs," but he will not part with it in spite of the tempting blandishments.

When Maeve's diplomatic attempts at capturing the bull fail, she sends out the armies of Connaught to secure it for her. The epic then moves through a fascinating labyrinth of plot and character, including flashbacks to the boyhood of the great mythic hero Cuchulainn (pronounced "Coo' culan," not "Cuckulainn" as I once did, and was never allowed to forget by my gleeful Irish friends).

In a mystical finale, the Brown Bull of Cooley and the White-Horned Bull of Connaught clash in a night of mighty combat with all Ireland the battlefield. In the morning the Brown Bull appears on the plains of Rathcroghan with the carcass of the White-Horned Bull upon his horns. Mortally wounded himself, the victor journeys to Cooley to die, and at each place he passes he leaves a part of the carcass of the White-Horned Bull, thus giving each place its name.

In Celtic mythology the queen represented the land itself, and when the king married her, it was through his nuptial vows and bed that he took symbolic sovereignty of the land, a concept that is obviously a fertility ritual.

Steeped in the heroic Celtic myths, Yeats took upon himself the mantle of the ancient Irish tradition of poet-mystic and gave his country an updated female persona for the land—Cathleen ni Houlihan, ". . . and she had the walk of a Queen." For Yeats she was not the "mother" but a young girl who symbolized the recovery of spirit and dignity for Ireland. The play, written in 1902, became a revolutionary rallying point, causing Yeats himself to wonder after 1916, "Did that play of mine send out/Certain men the English shot?"

Yeats is echoing the age-old, human, and particularly Irish preoccupation with martyrdom, with blood sacrifice, with the woman left bereft, which has its beginnings deep in Irish history and legend. It is on the slopes of Benbulben, overlooking his grave, that one such legend has its tragic denouement.

It is a tale that belongs to the saga of the Fianna, a band of superheroes led by the fabled giant Finn MacCool. Diarmuid of the "Love Spot" had earned the enmity of Finn MacCool by eloping with his bride to be, Grania, on the eve of their wedding, robbing Finn not only of pride but of his position as sovereign. For sixteen years Grania and Diarmuid lived the life of exiles. Finally, peace was made, but Finn's heart still could not forgive them.

By a trick, he involved Diarmuid in a hunt for an enchanted boar. Diarmuid found and slew the boar on the slopes of Benbulben, but not before, as had been foretold, the boar sprang upon him and tore out his bowels in a mortal wound.

The only thing that could have restored Diarmuid to life was water brought in the cupped hands of Finn MacCool, who had the magic power of healing. Three times Finn went to the well to bring the life-giving water, and each time he thought of Grania and let the water flow away through his fingers. The third time it was too late—Diarmuid's life had ebbed away. His friends covered his body with their cloaks and took his hound back to Grania that she might know he had been slain.

According to Yeats, the fierce warriors of the Fianna still haunt Benbulben: under the limestone, altarlike head of the mountain is a door and ". . . in the middle of the night it swings open and those wild unchristian riders rush forth upon the fields."

THE YEATS TAVERN
On the Bridge

Yeats Tavern—take a break reads the sign by the road. The Yeats Tavern commercializes Yeats outrageously, but so naïvely and with such sincere good nature that the only response possible is a smile.

The tavern is a roomy, two-story farmhouse. In the main room, over a raised platform used for musicians, is an enormous mural crudely depicting Lough Gill, over which floats, among pink clouds and swans, the disembodied head of Yeats himself, horn-rimmed specs, neatly combed hair, and all. Directly below him is a multi-colored jukebox.

The room is large and functional, the furniture worn. There's a pool table, and through a counter window opening into the kitchen you can receive a good, simple soup and plain sandwiches.

On the way out, you can pick up a little brochure entitled *Guide to the Yeats Country,* which, with its charmingly crude drawings, maps, history, and a few lines from Yeats's work, is worth the few pence it will cost you.

COUNTY ROSCOMMON

Roscommon County is what even the Irish refer to as "back of beyond." When someone expresses a need to get away from it all, the Irish will refer him or her with a laugh and a wink to Roscommon. It is an inland county where the main attraction is the beauty of the many island-dotted lakes that drowse in a countryside of level plains, bogland, river meadow, and low hills.

The main towns of Roscommon are Roscommon and Boyle.

AROUND ROSCOMMON

At eight miles on the road from town northwest to Castlerea, take a right to visit the castle at Ballintober. It's an imposing ruin and was the seat of the famous O'Connors of Connaught.

AROUND BOYLE

Two miles northeast of Boyle in the Rockingham demesne is Lough Key Forest Park, a good place for a walk and a picnic. On an island in the lake are the ruins of the Abbey of Trinity. Here medieval monks once compiled a local history, and in the shadow of its walls are the graves of Tomas Costello and Una MacDermot, an Irish Romeo and Juliet. After Una died, Tomas wrote for her one of the most beautiful love songs in any language: "Oh, fair Una, like a rose in a garden you,/ And like a candlestick of gold you were on/The table of a queen. . . ."

On the north side of the town of Boyle are the ruins of Boyle Abbey, Connaught's most important medieval abbey.

Midway between Carrick and Boyle is Cootehall, where the writer John McGahern grew up. His early novels deal with the realities of life in the west with a hard yet tender honesty that until recently caused his books to be banned. He is a master at evoking the rain-soaked and lonely landscape of Roscommon and the intricacies of parent-child relationships. McGahern presently lives in Carrick-on-Shannon, just across the border in Leitrim.

A country pub in Ireland is likely to be a naked barn of a room, with uncomfortable chairs and stools, plastic tabletops ringed and grimed by the stains of last night's pints and bottles. But if a voice, near closing time, is raised in song, the room will be transformed, a melody intricate in its simplicity moving through the fog of cigarette and pipe smoke.

—Thomas Flanagan

THE FOUR PROVINCES
On the Boyle–Croghan road

This pub, out in the middle of nowhere about five miles from Boyle, attracts large numbers of people from miles around. It is a real country pub, with a small bar, a stage for musicians, and a back room that is opened up for nights when there is dancing. Live music four nights a week.

ULSTER

County Antrim

County Derry

County Donegal

County Tyrone

County Fermanagh

County Armagh

County Monaghan

County Cavan

County Down

Ireland is Ireland through joy and through tears.
—Ninth-century ballad

British Northern Ireland comprises six counties of the province of Ulster (Antrim, Down, Armagh, Londonderry, Tyrone, and Fermanagh). The other three counties of Ulster (Donegal, Cavan, and Monaghan) are geographically northern but politically part of the Republic of Ireland.

Northern Ireland—these are words that bear a heavy load of association and emotional content. The political situation in Ulster today is immensely complex, with roots that reach deep into the Irish past and, indeed, into the common past of us all.

In Ireland, the struggle that divides her people is so starkly and clearly delineated that it can be seen as a metaphor for embattled humanity throughout the ages. The anguish of the seemingly insoluble "Irish problem" is the anguish of a world constantly warring yet searching for the solutions that will bring about global peace.

The present standoff in the North is too complicated for me to do anything in this book but provide the barest essentials of historical fact as background. For greater depth and detail I'd like to recommend: *A Concise History of Ireland* by Maire and Conor Cruise O'Brien (Thames and Hudson, 1972); *The Damnable Question* by George Dangerfield (Atlantic–Little, Brown, 1976); *A Place Apart* by Dervla Murphy (Devin-Adair and Penguin Books, 1978); *Too Long a Sacrifice* by Jack Holland (Penguin Books, 1982); and *A Short History of Ireland* by James C. Beckett (Hutchinson, 1975).

It all started in the eleventh century. At the invitation of Dermot, a disgruntled Irish king, the Normans, in the person of Strongbow and his army, arrived on Ireland's shore. This meant an English force was now at play in Ireland, for the Normans had subdued England in 1066.

But though the Normans won battles and established themselves on the land, they were not able to subdue Ireland. Conflict continued. Like the Vikings before them, the Normans were not immune to the magic of the Gaelic culture. By the fifteenth century they had been assimilated by those they would conquer.

To halt this trend, the English crown decided to reassert its claim to Ireland. Henry VIII installed officials there and sent troops to back them up. In 1541 he was declared King of Ireland. Decades of war ensued, complicated by Protestant versus Catholic in the English succession of monarchs. But by 1600 Ireland was firmly under England's domination.

The Irish earls who had fought bitterly to hold their land were decisively defeated in 1602. They fled into exile—"The Flight of the Earls." The English continued their policy of "plantation," giving the confiscated land of the Irish nobility to British and Scottish subjects.

In 1607 James I began the wholesale plantation of Ulster, the land that had once belonged to the particularly powerful and rebellious Hugh O'Neill, known as the Great O'Neill. Scots were imported to accomplish the feat, and a barony with title could be had for £1,000 by any Englishman who had it to spare.

The indefatigable O'Neill clan, led by Owen Roe O'Neill, returned from the Continent in 1641 to take part in the Catholic peasant rising that was marked by the massacre of Presbyterians (the Scots who had settled their land). When, in 1649, Oliver Cromwell overthrew the English crown, he wreaked a terrible revenge on all of Ireland. With his troops, he leveled the countryside, burning, killing, and pillaging as he went. Cromwell then instituted a reign of repression that continued to foster further plantation of Irish lands by the English.

In 1685 James II ascended the English throne, returning the monarchy to Catholicism. This threw Parliament into crisis and raised the hopes of the native Irish Catholic population that plantation would be abolished. But the Protestant Dutchman William of Orange came to

England to claim the throne and received the support of the establishment.

James II fled first to France, and then to Ireland, mustering his forces in Ulster. On July 1, 1690, at the Battle of the Boyne, Catholic James was defeated by Protestant Billy, and some 15,000 of Ireland's best fighting men went into exile in what is called the "Flight of the Wild Geese." Now Catholic native Ireland was totally subjugated by Protestant England.

The next two hundred years were given over to Anglo-Protestant Ascendancy. But once again the Irish culture worked its charm, and young Ascendancy aristocrats, identifying themselves as Irish and fired by the French Revolution, staged a rebellion in 1798. Rebellions and risings continued to bubble up, failing and yet gradually, bit by bit, regaining Irish rights—1848, 1867, 1879, and finally Easter 1916.

Five years of armed strife followed the Easter rebellion, and then, in 1922, the Irish Free State was declared, immediately embroiling Ireland in a civil war. A tentative solution was found in 1925, when predominantly Protestant Ulster (where the major plantations had been concentrated) was partitioned from the Irish Free State.

Finally, in 1949, the Republic of Ireland was born of the Irish Free State, but the island remains divided between the predominantly Catholic Republic in the South and Ulster in the North, predominantly British and Protestant.

In the present era, the violence that first flared here in 1968 has changed from a civil rights movement of the oppressed Catholic minority to a tragic tapestry of internecine warfare. England sent in troops to keep the peace, but their presence has served to further complicate matters.

The IRA, the British Army, the Royal Ulster constabulary (RUC, Northern Irish Police), and Protestant paramilitary organizations have all been guilty of outrages in Northern Ireland. Each new atrocity committed by one side was soon matched by a counterhorror on the other. Finally, for the populace caught in this web, the word became "resignation." The biggest problems for the Catholic minority continue to be the twin evils of joblessness and hopelessness. The struggle continued when the IRA brought the hunger strike, a new method based in ancient Celtic tradition, to bear on the British government.

While the situation itself remains tragic for many natives, especially in Belfast, the stranger traveling through the North has little more to fear at this time than the random violence he would encounter anywhere. Outside Belfast partisan violence is most often directed at specific targets, which does not involve the visitor.

As you wander through the rich, verdant countryside of the North, the very idea of battle recedes until it assumes the properties of a dream, its ugly reality becoming, as always, theoretical to all except those who must live it. Fear of this reality should not prevent the visitor from experiencing the earthy marvels of the North, which predate and will outlast all human strife: the nine Glens of Antrim, the strange phenomenon of the Giant's Causeway, the salmon-filled lakes, the perfect deserted beaches and bright-green hills, dotted with lambs, that roll to the edge of cliffs or straight to the sea.

Here, safe in a landscape of ancient peace and kind people, the bitterness of the Irish struggle, so near and yet so far, is strangely highlighted. Perhaps you can begin to understand it and its deeper implications.

In the last decade, foreigners anxious about the war have avoided the North, leaving it mostly unspoiled by that creeping blight that must be fought in the South—"plasticization." The foreign traveler is a rare sight, so the country people take particular pleasure in talking to you. They will speak to you in their flat Northern lilt, with just a hint of a Scots burr, sprinkling the language with words like "wee" and "bairn" (child). You'll feel a more serious overall tone here than in the South. The humor has more sarcasm, the architecture in the towns is heavier and more darkly Victorian, the streets wider. To offset this tendency toward the dour, the countryside is blessed with some of the most luminous and opalescent skies in the world.

Pub life is timeless, inbred, regional, with much room for eccentricity, and plenty of good food. The favorite drink aside from Guinness is Black Bush, Irish whiskey that is distilled in Bushmills, County Antrim. Warning: Black Bush may be habit-forming. I found it so.

Hours: 11:00 a.m. to 11:00 p.m. six days a week. All pubs are closed on Sundays, though you can order a drink in your hotel room.

COUNTY ANTRIM

Antrim forms the northeast corner of Ireland; on a clear day Scotland can be seen from any point on the Antrim coast. Much of the character of the country—the cottages, shops, churches, and villages—has a distinctly Scottish flavor.

Antrim is justly famous for a number of natural wonders; there's the twisting splendor of the Antrim Coast Road, the nine flowery glens, the miraculous Giant's Causeway, and Bushmills Whiskey.

CAUSEWAY HOTEL
Vicinity Bushmills

Fortunately for the traveler, there's a spot where two of these wonders can be experienced simultaneously. Go to the bar of the Causeway Hotel and order a Black Bush. This wonderful, old, gabled Victorian edifice can be reached either from the road leading from Bushmills to the coast or from the cliff walk with its fresh sea winds and astounding views.

I stumbled upon the hotel by accident. Out for a walk along the road, I came upon a man and a boy bearing fishing poles. I followed them, keeping a few shy paces behind, in the hope that they would lead me to an interesting spot. We walked through green fields, surprising the sheep. The breeze smelled of the sea—and suddenly, between two hills, blue water. It was then that I got a good look at the man. In the place where one of his eyes should have been was a hole. Perhaps it was not a scar of war, but to me it was a reminder, on this timeless shore, of that other world of men and bloodshed.

I walked along the flowery path at the edge of the cliff, alone except for an occasional sightseer. Rounding a bend, I gazed down at the strange formation called the Giant's Causeway. It is a sea of prismatic columns forming a sort of uneven "yellow brick road." Legend has it that it's the work of the heroic warrior of Irish mythology, Finn Mac-Cool, who created it for his use as steppingstones to Scotland. Those more scientifically minded say it was caused 60 million years ago by a curious cooling (MacCooling?) of a basalt-based volcanic outflow.

Take your pick, or, since you are in the paradoxical world of Ireland, believe both.

As I came up some wooden steps from the viewing point, my interest was caught by an eroding sign with an arrow: CAUSEWAY HOTEL. The arrow pointed straight into a flowering hedge. Looking closer, I saw an overgrown path tunneling through the fragrant foliage.

Unable to resist this fairy-tale appeal, I entered the green tunnel, to emerge in full sunshine before a rambling Victorian house surrounded by rolling green meadows and facing the ocean. I had walked onto the cover of a gothic novel.

The interior was no disappointment. A large central hallway with a graceful staircase that sailed up to a mezzanine was softly lit by milky skylights. The original furnishings had survived: carved Victorian chairs and chests, sets of gazelle horns, hunting and fishing prints, portraits of famous dogs and horses, glazed-eyed deer heads, unwilling trophies of the hunts of long ago. The walls were painted a warm, light shade called Malahide orange, a color invented in the eighteenth century for Malahide Castle just outside of Dublin.

I made my way to the bar—a small, cozy back room with a ceiling and bar of pressed tin, and the usual overall tone of brown. Over the bar was a painting of a very thin and disdainful-looking greyhound, who, I learned, was the prize-winning Master McGrath. The TV was off and there was a fire going. A few people were sitting at small tables exchanging gossip. I ordered a Black Bush.

Soup and sandwiches are available in the wood-paneled lounge, and a fine meal is served in the dining room overlooking the sea.

OF SPECIAL INTEREST

OLD BUSHMILLS DISTILLERY
Bushmills

A telephone call in advance to Bushmills 31521 is necessary to arrange a visit to the world's oldest distillery (founded 1603). The pure (unblended) ten-year-old liqueur (famous the world over as Black Bush) can be sampled in a visitor's bar decorated with historical references.

Whiskey from Old Bushmills is a blend of a single malt and a single grain. In fact, the agriculture of the area is keyed to the needs of the distillery. The local barley is especially peated to the distillery's rigid specification, and the water comes from St. Columb's Rill, a tributary of the adjacent river Bush. The water has a "character," rising from peaty ground and thence flowing over basalt. The result is a whiskey that is one of the finest in the world.

Not far from Bushmills is Dunluce Castle, which stands on an isolated crag above the sea. Its name roughly translates from the Gaelic as "Mermaid's Fort," and the waterfront tower is called Maeve Roe's Tower. The castle was the home of the MacQuillans and Maeve was their banshee. She is said to sweep the tower at night.

BELFAST

When people are deeply unsure of themselves, when their past has to be constantly invoked to explain or excuse their present and when nothing about their future is known or can safely be predicted, a sort of intellectual ferment starts; and not merely, or even chiefly, in academic or literary circles. All over Northern Ireland ordinary people are trying to think their own way through The Problem and this personal sorting-out process marks one of the most obvious differences between North and South.

—Dervla Murphy

My name is O'Hanlon, I'm just gone sixteen.
My home is in Monaghan, there I was weaned.
I learned all my life, cruel England to blame
And so I'm a part of the Patriot Game.

—Dominic Behan

The basic fear of the Protestants in Northern Ireland is that they will be outbred by the Roman Catholics.

—Lord O'Neill
(Former Prime Minister)

Belfast sits in its encircling ring of hills like a dark stone in a brilliant setting. To the east is the deep coastal inlet of Belfast Lough.

Arriving in this city of bewildering and violent crosscurrents and contradictions is like being thrust straight into the heart of human conflict. Even for the visitor prepared by media, the realities that face a Belfast inhabitant are an emotional and physical shock.

Imagine being unable to visit your friends across town without incurring danger. Imagine your children afraid to walk by parked cars. Imagine six-year-olds on missions of destructive vandalism. Imagine areas where the police never come because they would face immediate death. Imagine large numbers of heavily armed troops constantly patrolling your town. Imagine the center of the town sealed off so that to go shopping you must pass through checkpoints where your person and belongings are searched by uniformed men and women, or streets of working-class homes barricaded with high brick and corrugated walls separating neighbors so that they will not be provoked into killing or hurting each other.

These are the elements that form your first impressions and leave you with a feeling of imbalance and paranoia. But though your senses can never fully relax, after the initial shock you do begin to experience another Belfast.

Somber Victorian buildings enlivened with cherubs and reliefs of Greek gods, Indians, Chinese, and historical personages stand regally among new brick-and-glass buildings, cobbled pedestrian malls, and flowered parks. The shells of bombed and ruined houses are being rebuilt. Off in the distance, visible from almost every street, Cave Hill presents its famous profile (some say it's Napoleon).

Belfast's history is one of growth as fast and surprising as mushrooms after a rain. In the seventeenth century Belfast was a village. Then shipbuilding, seaborne commerce, linen, engineering, tobacco, and other industries resulted in the town's doubling in size every ten years.

By the end of the century the population of Belfast had grown to 2,000—a fourfold increase since 1600. The city's prosperity continued into the next century, but along with it came a growing resentment among the townsfolk against the English policy of repression.

The Society of United Irishmen was founded in 1791, when Wolfe Tone, Samuel Nielson, Thomas Russell, Henry Joy McCracken, and Henry Spiers climbed Cave Hill and there pledged themselves to Irish independence. McCracken led the insurgents at the Battle of Antrim in 1798, and was hanged at Corn Market on Belfast's High Street.

Side by side with these developments went a cultural revival, and the Belfast of the late eighteenth and early nineteenth centuries has been dubbed, because of its enlightenment, the "Athens of the North."

In 1862, Harland and Wolff was founded, a firm that was to build some of the world's largest ships. Even today, the twin Goliath cranes of Harland and Wolff dominate the Belfast skyline. New machinery and processes also helped Belfast to a position of supremacy in the linen industry, and in the nineteenth century the population jumped from 25,000 to 300,000.

The people of Belfast are a tough lot and have a particular sharp humor born of the "Problem," in which they have found themselves encapsulated for so long. It is deceptively easy to escape Belfast and leave it all behind. Buses can take you to a beautiful countryside only half an hour away. I took one of these buses to the Belfast zoo one sunny Sunday afternoon. The zoo is laid out in tiers on the side of a hill, and the Sunday crowd climbed around eating candy, pushing strollers with babies, and marveling at the strange creatures in their cages. Down below us Belfast glinted in the sun.

Such a sense of schizophrenia is what Belfast is all about. In the twinkling of an eye you can find peace—in the wondrous Botanical Gardens, in the Linenhall Library, where history resides in the hushed old rooms, or on the traditional mock-Tudor campus of Queen's University, the center of learning for Northern Ireland. The museum is full of the reclaimed treasures of the ancient Celtic peoples, and the Belfast intelligentsia, whether their surnames are Protestant or Catholic, have an objectivity and painful wit about their situation and that of humankind that has been refined by suffering into a Belfast specialty.

But in the Catholic Falls area and the Protestant Shankill section, fear and privation, physical and spiritual, continue.

War numbs those it does not kill. Feelings that have to cope with violent death on a daily basis soon become exhausted—there is only so much tragedy and horror a person can deal with, whilst still going about his or her everyday life. In order to survive, they must withdraw from the tragedy, suppress the grief. But no one ever really forgets.

—Jack Holland
Letters from a Belfast Ghetto

THE CROWN LIQUOR SALOON
Great Victoria Street
This is an extraordinarily well-preserved saloon, almost cathedral-like, with stained glass, a floor of mosaic tiles, a great stone fireplace, and brocaded walls. The intricately carved snugs are in mint condition, and only the color TV intrudes on a scene that otherwise has remained unchanged for a century.

W. & A. GILBEY
Corn Market
You enter this wine merchant's shop, pass through to the elevator, and press the button marked BAR. You will emerge in a small room with comfortable chairs and the atmosphere of a club. Here gather the regulars in the wine trade and a number of Ulster personalities.

KELLY'S CELLARS
Bank Lane
Henry Joy McCracken, the United Irishman, hid under the counter from the Redcoats, and Joe Devlin, a member of both the British and North Irish Parliaments, served the licensed trade. The downstairs bar has a low, well-scrubbed counter, nice snugs, and walls decorated with scenes of old Belfast.

THE ULSTER WINE STORES BLOUSE BAR
North Street through the Ulster Wine Store
Pass through the off-license "ladies only" room, where stout elderly women sit together drinking their companionable pints at wooden tables. Through the doors, at the back, is the Red Hand (symbol of Ulster), a large, high-ceilinged room with walls covered with marvelous old sporting photographs. The drinking here is quiet and peaceful, and over the bar is written:

> *This bar is dedicated to those splendid*
> *fellows who make drinking a pleasure,*
> *who reach content prior to capacity*
> *who can take what they drink,*
> *hold it, enjoy it, and remain upright.*

The people at the Northern Irish Tourist Board are very helpful. If you have questions or need help, they are located at River House, 48 High Street, Belfast.

CUSHENDALL

MARY MacNEILL'S
Cushendall, in the heart of the Glens of Antrim, is the capital of the Glens. Nearby is the sandstone Curfew Tower (once a jail), and just behind the village is Tiveragh Hill. If you're walking on the hill just at twilight and hear faint music coming from a crevice, it's either one Black Bush too many or it's the fairies who are supposed to dwell in a palace there.

Mary MacNeill's is one of the smallest pubs in Ireland, partly filled by the bulk of Mary, who is the repository of all the gossip of the relatively isolated and beautiful valleys in the surrounding neighborhood. Her pub serves as a local news exchange where everyone drops in for the latest word and a good chat and visitors are welcome for what they can report of the world outside.

LARA LODGE
Glenariff Forest Park
Glenariff was described by Thackeray as "Switzerland in miniature," and he was right: waterfalls, cool ferny dells, and flowering meadows.

Lara Lodge is a rustic hostelry at the lower end of a ravishing path up the glen to a nature museum and viewpoint. Stop here for refreshment.

PORTGLENONE

CROSSKEYS INN
I was told of this pub by several Irish friends whose taste in pubs is impeccable and whose knowledge of same is indisputable, but when Davy Hammond, the well-known Belfast balladeer said it was a good place for music, I was certain it had to be special.

And special it is, for it is the Mecca for Ulster practitioners of traditional music and ballads. The owner, Sean Stinson, weaves a warm atmosphere and welcomes converts to the eloquence of Irish music.

The setting for the music is perfect—an old country pub once a coaching stop, with thatched roof and turf fires, situated near Lough Neagh and the broad river Bann.

Lough Neagh harbors many legends, as does almost every part of the Irish landscape. Beneath its waters, which are reputed to be able to turn wood into stone, there lies a town, it is said. The magic lake was created, goes the story, when the giant Finn MacCool grabbed two handfuls of earth to fling at an enemy. The place where he dug filled up and became Lough Neagh, and the two fistfuls of earth became the Isle of Man.

> On Lough Neagh's banks as the fisherman strays,
> In the clear cool eve declining,
> He sees the round towers of other days
> In the waves beneath him shining. . . .
> —Thomas Moore

TEMPLEPATRICK

DUNADRY INN

This is a converted linen mill. As it is five miles from Belfast Airport (Aldergrove), it is a good place for a drink before arriving or departing. There are frequent displays of Ulster-manufactured goods (at which exporters and importers meet) and evening entertainments. The all-round standard is good.

COUNTY DERRY

> If the whole of Scotland were mine
> From the center of the sea
> I would prefer a home
> In the middle of gentle Derry.
>
> No leaf falls on the ground
> In beautiful, most lovely Derry
> Without two virgin angels
> To guard it as it lies.

> *The seagulls of Lough Foyle*
> *Fly above me as I go*
> *But even they will not come with me*
> *Sad my exile from Derry.*
>
> *With the cries I hear*
> *How can I survive*
> *The great cry of the Derry people*
> *Has broken my heart in four.*
>
> —St. Colmcille

The region from Strabane (Tyrone) to Maghera (Derry) is sometimes called "America's Home Counties," because it produced so many presidents, generals, and immigrants. They include General James Shields, who founded Portland, Oregon; President Ulysses S. Grant; and Charles Thomson, who drafted the American Declaration of Independence. Many country cottages in these parts have old American clocks, collector's pieces sent home long ago by emigrant sons.

The county of Derry is beautifully hilly, with a ridge of mountains, the Sperrins, rising up along the border of Tyrone and a marvelous Atlantic coastline of surf-washed beaches. Central to Derry is the city of Derry, commanding the surrounding countryside from a hill overlooking a broad tidal curve of the river Foyle.

DERRY CITY

> Despite Derry's splendid setting, one's first impression is of physical squalor. Uninspired new buildings contrast with scenes of destruction, demolition, reconstruction—and bare ugly sites awaiting further uninspired buildings. But this morning, as I explored many hilly streets, unexpected laneways and attractive unbombed corners, I found some ancient spell being laid upon me.
>
> —Dervla Murphy

A thousand years before the English came, Derry was founded by St. Colmcille on a tree-crowned hill. Here at Doire (the oak grove) he built his favorite monastery. Since then Derry has been battled over countless times and withstood two famous sieges, thus earning her title of the "Maiden City."

Derry did not actually become a city till 1614, when a group of London guilds provided labor and cash for the creation of the last walled city to be built in Europe.

Today, modern Derry is undergoing another kind of siege. For the stranger it begins at the approach to the bridge. Not only are passports and luggage checked by an armed soldier alongside a policeman but detailed questions are asked the visitor—where is he coming from? where will he be staying?

As in Belfast, armed foot patrols of British soldiers and vehicles full of Brits pointing rifles have become everyday reality to the Derry citizenry. But "Derry is different," the inhabitants tell writer Dervla Murphy, who goes on to observe, "By which they mean that Derry people, whatever their religion or politics, are not temperamentally inclined toward Belfast's brand of implacable sectarianism."

Dervla Murphy is the author of a remarkable book on the North, A Place Apart. Her viewpoint is unique. The author hails from Waterford in the Republic, and her Southern status places her in the strange position of being both an insider and an outsider. Traveling through the countryside on a bicycle named Roz, she succeeded in speaking directly to the people of the North—both Protestant (orange) and Catholic (green)—and recorded their environment and varied voices, plus her own responses, with acuity and warmth.

Derry is built on both sides of the river Foyle, four miles upstream from the broad Atlantic inlet of Lough Foyle. Houses, churches, shops, and ruins rise in tiers on the steep embankments. Spanning the river is Craigavon Bridge, a double-decker expanse of steel that joins more than just opposite sides of the Foyle. The bridge connects Waterside, the largely Protestant area, to the old walled city, and to the Bogside, Creggan, and Brandywell, the Catholic areas.

The Bogside, a government-built housing estate, is so called because it was erected on filled-in swampland just outside the original walls of the city. I went to the Bogside armed with the name and address of a relative of John Hume, a prominent political figure, and the name of a good pub, the Rockingchair. Walking through the geometrically laid-out streets bare of traffic and trees, I tried to ignore the suspicious stares that greeted my progress past the small houses, some with flower gardens and miniature rose bushes.

Strangers stick out here like the proverbial sore thumb, and I must have looked uneasy and lost, because a friendly voice called down to me from a second-story balcony, "Are ye looking for someone?" I replied that I was looking for the Rockingchair Pub.

"You shouldna be goin' there. It's not a good place atall," disapproved the owner of the voice, a heavy-set matron with curly hair. "Where are ye from?"

"New York."

"Ah, New York. Why don't you come up ta me for some tay," she said, and with that disappeared inside.

I had the tea while we chatted and she washed her kitchen floor. The place was tiny and filled with the usual knickknacks: photographs of family, religious pictures, and, as in many Irish homes, a heroic painting of John and Robert Kennedy. I told her who I was looking for in the Bogside, and she clasped her hands in pleasured wonder. "John Hume. Oh, John's my cousin," she said. She rushed out on the balcony and called out to the women who were sitting in front of their houses. "Come up. There's a girl here from New York." In a few minutes I was surrounded by friendly faces and questioning Northern voices.

The Rockingchair turned out to be the other side of hospitality. The barman showed no inclination to talk, and though I was the object of twenty-five to thirty pairs of eyes, I was coolly ignored. I had stumbled into the favorite haunt of the Provos (radical IRA). The tense, suspicious atmosphere brought me to a point of paranoia that made me drink down my pint fast and get out.

At night, the center of town is closed off and life flows on around the city's temporarily hollow hub. I stood outside the barbed wire and wondered what to do next. From across the river came loud booms. Gunfire?

Three teenage boys and a girl were walking toward me. "What are ye doin' down here, then?" said the tallest boy. I told them I was looking for a friendly pub. Minutes later I was driving across the bridge with them to their home ground in Waterside. The cannon-like booms were drums, they explained. This day was the twelfth of July, the special day when all of Protestant Northern Ireland heat themselves up in frenzied

celebration of King Billy's long-ago victory at the Battle of the Boyne.

The drums, called Lambeg drums, are large skin-covered instruments slung from the neck and carried sideways. They are beaten with sticks attached with thongs to the drummer's wrists. Sometimes the straps dig into the player's flesh after many hours of playing and his drum is spattered with his own blood. This is considered a proud sign of the drummer's dedication and patriotism.

We drove to a square with a children's playground. A huge bonfire blazed away; about forty people were standing around talking, their faces lit by the flames. Battle songs rang out, and the silhouette of a child on a swing flew back and forth, a dark shadow across the fiery background.

My new friends and I sat in a row on the curbstone. "Will ye take me to New York?" asked one of them. His friend immediately grabbed him by the shirt. "I'm the one who'll be goin'," he said menacingly. " 'Twas my idea to ask her." Here all Americans are seen as rich, and most teenagers are desperate to leave. "There's nothing here," they say. But there is something special about Derry, and once they've left, the young become nostalgic.

As I cycled past one patrol, under a deep blue sky with the sun glinting merrily on the glass splinters strewn across the street, I suddenly felt nauseated by the sheer mindlessness of the violence that has erupted here. That young Irishmen and young Englishmen should be trained to be able and willing to kill each other . . . seems intolerably barbarous. I've never been a pacifist but maybe Northern Ireland is making me one. . . .By 2076, will our legalised killings seem as outrageous to Europeans as hanging for the theft of a sheep seems now?

Fortunately these depressed moods never last long and I am on the whole finding Derry the reverse of gloomy. It seems exhilarating, stimulating and curiously exciting—almost intoxicating. . . .It is exciting not in any morbid sense (not nowadays) but as a city of lively people trying to restore their communal self-respect through their own efforts. Almost everybody I met has been involved in some sort of community work. . . .Any chance contact is liable to interrupt a sentence, look at his or her watch and disappear in a flurry of apologies to edit a community newspaper, or direct an interdenominational drama group, or attend a meeting on Summer Play Groups or Tenants' Rights or battered wives or homeless old people or deserted children or alcoholics or prostitutes. The Maiden City's recent ordeals have certainly not broken her spirit.

—Dervla Murphy

I did finally get to Derry's pubs. The proprietor of a music store where I went to buy a tin whistle closed up shop to take me on a friendly pub crawl. Though journalists are seen as exploiters in both Derry and Belfast, I was a writer, plus that oddity, a woman traveling alone, and I was treated with great kindness.

The following pubs are "very old" and comfortable.

WATERSIDE

THE BAT AND BALL
Bonds Hill (bottom)

CLASSIC BAR
Spencer Road

CITYSIDE

THE GLUE POT
Shipley Street

THE ANCHOR
Kerrykey

THE VICTORIA BAR
Orchard Street
Unique place; has no windows

Note: A beautiful thing to try to find to take home is one of the old stoneware bottles unique to Derry.

PORTSTEWART

Portstewart is a place for holidays. There are pools and coves and surf-washed sands that stretch nearly two miles from the cliffs south of the town. There are two 18-hole golf courses, tennis, boating, and sea fishing.

O'MALLEY'S
The Edgewater Beach

Although the hotel is only a half century old, it gives the impression of being an aged rural inn. Its bar faces off the tiny wood-paneled lobby toward a view of the magnificent ocean beach between the town and the river Bann. It's a favorite retreat for fishermen fresh from angling for sea bass, sea trout, porbeagle sharks, and tope.

MOYOLA PARK GOLFING COMPLEX
Castledawson

Food: Full menu   *Specialty:* Salami

Situated on the well-known trout and salmon river Moyola, and close to Lough Neagh, this new "open" club occupies part of the estate of a former Northern Ireland Prime Minister, Lord Moyola, who is keen on all sports and on rural development. A specialty is locally made Ulster salami. There is a restaurant attached, open on Sundays, and it affords the opportunity of grasping the Ulster semireligious golfing fever.

COUNTY DONEGAL

Donegal is the most northerly county in Ireland, stretching along much of the northwest coast. Because the county's foundation is a wild assortment of rock and stone, from cave-pocked limestone to mixtures of igneous, the scenery atop it is equally varied; sweet-smelling glens and meadows and the lushest of lush green farmland roll to the bare harshness of tumbling cliffs. Donegal offers a smiling countenance, especially in summer, bedecked with hydrangeas and wafting the perfumes of haymaking, turf smoke, and sea spray.

ARDARA

Ardara is the place to buy your homespun Donegal tweeds. They are made here. The town is a center, too, for hand knitting and embroidery, all of which you can watch. Hosiery is another specialty.

Ardara is prettily placed in a wide valley where the Owentocher River enters Loughros More Bay. Mahgera Caves, Essaranks Waterfall, and the Slievetooey Mountains, all to the west, make a nice day's outing. For a good view, go six miles to Loughros Point.

NANCY'S
Main Street

Nancy's is an old Victorian house filled with antiques. You may find yourself enjoying a drink in the company of a small group in the sitting room; then, as more people arrive, more rooms are opened up in a seemingly endless unfolding of hospitality. Nancy's should not be missed.

RATHMULLAN

Rathmullan is the kind of old-fashioned resort you associate with tea in ancient sea-front hotels, with sand castles, beach umbrellas, and rolled-up trouser legs. It is situated on the shores of Lough Swilly, a fjord-like arm of the sea that reaches inland for twenty-five miles. Rathmullan's strand is blessed with a series of sandy coves, like exclusive little stone-walled rooms, each with its own private portion of land and sea.

It was from one of these little sandy coves along Lough Swilly that the great lords of the North, the earls of Tir Conail and Tir Eoghain, fled into exile after the final defeat at Kinsale, when the "Wild Geese" of Ireland's military and aristocratic classes "spread grey wing on every tide."

Just across Lough Swilly at Buncrana another historic uprising came to ground. In October 1798, Wolfe Tone sailed into the sheltered inlet aboard the French battleship *Hoch* coming to the aid of the United Irishmen—but he was too late. The ship was captured and Tone arrested. He was sentenced to death, but committed suicide before the sentence could be carried out.

The British were not long in recognizing one of the world's finest natural harbors, and made Rathmullan the headquarters for their North Atlantic fleet. They built the excellent pier that still serves the town today, and left behind a wrecked ship (said to have carried bullion) at the mouth of the lough—to the joy of several generations of Rathmullan boys.

In the 1920s Rathmullan was a major fishing port where Russians came to buy the barrels of salted North Sea herring, and where buyers came from Cyprus and the Canaries to purchase Donegal seed potatoes, still considered to be Ireland's best.

THE PIER HOTEL

The Pier Hotel has sheltered its share of this colorful crowd of visitors. James Deeney, the proprietor, is the third generation to welcome strangers to the pier, and surely, of his five children, one will continue the tradition of friendly conversation and well-pulled pints. Steaks are good here, too.

For a special treat, try dinner at Rathmullan House, the former residence of a well-to-do Belfast family and now famous for its spectacular elegance, gardens, and food.

COUNTY TYRONE

AUGHER

JIMMY JOHNSTON'S

Here, in the Clogher Valley, you are in the heart of traditional Ulster—so Irish and yet so different from the South. "Protestant-looking," they would say here—meaning plain, practical, thorough. The visitors' book consists of thirteen volumes side by side, dating back to Jimmy's grandfather and earlier, and (never mind what you think of the pub) you are requested to put in your date and place of birth. Jimmy is overjoyed by strangers: an Eskimo or a Chinese would have too valuable an address to drink otherwise than on the house. Next door to the bar, a shop sells Augher cheese, wrapped attractively as bait for far-flung signatories in volumes 13 *et seq.* Down the road a bit is the birthplace of William Carleton, Ireland's Dostoevsky, novelist of the horrors and humors of poverty and ignorance.

THE BATTERY
On the western shores of Lough Neagh near
the Arboe High Cross

Though Tyrone is a Northern county, Irish-Gaelic roots are as plainly in evidence here and throughout the North as they are in the Republic. Along with the round tower and the harp, the high cross is a uniquely Irish creation and a symbol of the country's individuality.

The High Cross at Arboe is one of many across the land. There are more than 150 such monuments in churchyards, village streets, and even in open fields. Historians have enjoyed trying to explain the mystery of their haphazard distribution throughout the countryside: clusters of them in some areas, none at all in others.

The urge to create high crosses seems to have lasted from the eighth to the twelfth centuries. They are artifacts so intricate and lacy in their stonework that a writer could be tempted to follow suit in describing them. However, I will not succumb. Briefly: a high cross is a huge Celtic cross formed of the Christian cross with a circle surrounding the intersection of shaft and bar. An Irish friend of mine told me this represents the union of the cross and the sun, the union of Christian and pagan Ireland. It does seem like an accurate and concise way to illustrate what actually happened.

The crosses themselves were erected as monuments to victory over death—a celebration of the redemption of man by Christ. The scenes engraved on them were based on appropriate stories from the Bible, and the carving is alive with decorative detail: exquisitely molded spiral patterns often enlivened by birds' heads or other animal features; complex compositions of interlacing and knotted cords; the stylized bodies and limbs of men, animals, birds, and serpents. These motifs express a miraculous blend of Christian doctrine and pagan nature worship, something you'll find is still very real, though totally unself-conscious, in rural Ireland.

So go ahead and see the Arboe High Cross, an especially exciting version of these stone flights of the imagination, and afterward repair to The Battery for a pint and some good stories.

The Battery is an old barging stop; outside, you can stand on the quay, and imagine the barges wending their way down the river Bann to Portadown, Newry, and then Dublin. Proprietor Arthur Ryan will tell you all about it, or ask for that tough old bargee, Mrs. Tenneyson. The Battery is also the site of great eel fishing; eels can be lifted out of the lake in weirs 500 stone at a time. Appropriate reading: Seamus Heaney's "A Lough Neagh Sequence."

> Irish conversation was like one of those Celtic designs . . . made up of a simple form like a serpent that tied itself into a thousand ornamental knots before finally eating its own tail.

> —Patrick McGinley
> *Bogmail*

COUNTY FERMANAGH

Winding through the center of Fermanagh is the river Erne, which expands into Upper and Lower Lough Erne, two large and fish-filled bodies of water delightfully spotted with a plethora of islands.

ENNISKILLEN

The county town, Enniskillen, is cleverly situated at the point where the river separates into the two lakes.

In the seventeenth century, Enniskillen was one of the principal strongholds of the English and Scottish settlers, and the center of the corn and butter markets. Today it is noted for its handmade lace, sweaters, and china.

BLAKE'S OF THE HOLLOW
Church Street

In a maze of time-worn buildings stands Blake's, thought by some to be the best pub in Ulster, perhaps because of its lovingly cared-for Guinness. The exterior is still painted with red and black stripes, formerly for identification by peasants who could not read.

Blake's breathes the very essence of a Northern country pub, where men with seamed faces gather in the light of tinted globes to sip for hours in the tranquil silence. When last I was in Blake's there was no

TV to break the contemplative spell; it was switched on only for important sports events.

Coming into Blake's you leave the twentieth century behind except for the automatic drink dispensers on the bottles most frequently requested, which limit the bartender's ability to pour you a friendly "stiff one."

LISNASKEA

PAT CASSIDY'S PUBLIC HOUSE
AND FOLK MUSEUM
Main Street

This pub is the embodiment of the principle that a pub is the expression of the personality of its owner. Pat Cassidy, who owns and runs this one, is a bony sexagenarian with a hidden twinkle. He is a shanachie (a repository of myth and history, a chronicler and storyteller with special gifts) and museum curator. The pub is always buzzing with talk and laughter.

Mr. Cassidy is justifiably proud of his collection of incredibilia, which is housed on shelves behind the bar and also in a cram-packed back room.

Looking around this room you know immediately that you'll never be able to examine the cornucopia of objects in one visit: ancient farm implements, old stoves, a scarecrow made of wicker, a rocking chair fashioned from roots, handmade fish traps, a ladder two meters long, a yellowing photograph of a man seven feet tall, stuffed animals, etc., etc., etc.

Patrick Cassidy and his collection are famous. He has appeared in numerous magazine and newspaper articles and on radio and television. Anthropological types come to tape his folk stories and reminiscences.

Pat holds forth from behind the bar, sometimes enthroned in a shabby but comfortable armchair. He doesn't just tell a story, he orchestrates it. From his vast store of oddities he will bring up something—a small donkey made of bottle caps, a salmon stuffed one hundred years ago (as you can tell at a glance), a pair of gigantic boots about size 20. Using one of these as a starting point, he weaves his story like a spell, drawing everyone at the bar into it.

"These boots," he says, "belonged to a giant named John. He always worked with a real little fella. Well, the little fella got so used to being with John and doing what he did that when John ducked his head to go through a door, why the little fella'd duck his head, too."

"I know that," chimes in a voice at the bar. "I remember playing cards with those two. The big fella could see everyone's cards he was that tall, and then he'd signal to the little fella."

Pat goes on to tell how John, so visible in any crowd, was always in demand as a standard-bearer in parades. Protestant or Catholic, no parade was complete without him, and though he himself was a Catholic, John did not find it strange to march under a Protestant banner. Parades were all just celebrations.

Pat Cassidy is also an expert on folk tradition. Pulling out a fairly repulsive goat's foot, he dangles it casually while recounting how country people used to hang one in the chimney in order to ward off the evil eye.

He moves with complete ease from one topic to another, censoring himself when he feels he has made a wrong move and flowing smoothly on to another subject. "Ghosts," he says to me, "what do you think about ghosts?" For some reason, perhaps because he didn't like my reply, he refused to talk further about ghosts but simply changed the topic. I tried to steer him back, but he refused to acknowledge that he'd ever mentioned them at all.

In this pub, I witnessed an example of typical Irish subtlety. A traveling salesman had come in for his pint and was being rather a "city dandy." Everyone, including Pat, pointedly stopped talking till the cool atmosphere forced him to leave. This pub is indeed, as an Irish friend of mine put it, "freakishly Irish. Friendly. They'll debate everything including you."

COUNTY ARMAGH

Armagh is called the border of Ulster, for obvious reasons. A rich, fruit-growing area, it's a good place to be in blossom time. Much flax is also grown in this county, Lurgan and Portadown being important centers of the linen industry.

PORTADOWN

Nicely situated in the center of Armagh's apple-growing country, Portadown is probably the most typically Protestant town in the Ulster county that saw the birth of the ultra-Protestant "Orange Order." Portadown is a railway junction for the main lines linking Dublin, Belfast, Derry, Armagh, and the North Midlands. It is also a bustling industrial center.

McCONVILLE'S
West Street
Among all the hustle of business, McConville's has endured unchanged, a genuine old Victorian pub in the great tradition of elaborate snugs and rich decoration.

After you've snugged your fill, go over to the Green Garter, also on West Street, for an excellent meal. The proprietress, Mrs. Mae Noble, prides herself on being able to fix you whatever your heart desires (barring anything *too* outrageous).

COUNTY MONAGHAN

Monaghan is a county formed of many small hills—as though the land were frozen waves of green and tilled fields. This county is famous for coarse fishing and also for the clan of MacMahon, which was powerful in this territory.

EMYVALE

Emyvale is in the heart of a wonderfully wooded area. Close by is Lough Emy, a favorite haunt for a wide variety of wild fowl and swans.

THE EMYVALE INN

The Emyvale Inn is a rather small Old World type of pub, decorated with horse tackle and stuffed animal heads. It is quiet and comfortable.

COUNTY DOWN

This county is one of the most fertile in Ireland, and the gentle, beautifully cultivated hills rise in low swells like some idyllic, half-remembered illustration from a children's book. It is also the most populous of the Ulster counties, with fine roads connecting the resorts that dot the winding coast. The county includes the part of Belfast that lies east of the river Lagan.

BALLOO

BALLOO HOUSE

Balloo is fifteen miles southeast of Belfast and two miles from Whiterock, Ulster's biggest sailing and cruising center, on Strangford Lough. The big Georgian converted farmhouse is a rallying center for the huntin', fishin', sailin', motorin' crowd. East Down staghounds sometimes meet here. The clientele is composed mainly of hearty gentry, and the atmosphere is boisterous and good-natured. This is a place to meet Unionists at play.

CRAWFORDSBURN

CRAWFORDSBURN INN

Along the route on the south shore of the Belfast Lough, between Holywood and Bangor, lies Crawfordsburn Inn, one of the oldest coaching respites in the British Isles. Captain Josias Bodley, who stopped here in 1603, said in his diary that he could choose from a large and beautiful cellar Muscatel wine, stuffed geese, venison pies, and various other types of game and French dishes known as kickshaws (a rough translation of *quelque chose*).

Crawfordsburn has survived four centuries of tempestuous Irish history. It comes complete with a majestic stone fireplace, great oak beams, stone-flagged floors, low ceilings, brandy kegs, and a magnificent chandelier all tucked away under a thatched roof.

The local drinks in those olden times were "syllabub," a mixture of sweet wine and cream; "mum," a beer brewed from wheat; and "buttered ale," beer served hot and flavored with cinnamon and butter. The choices today at the bar are less esoteric—and certainly more expensive.

CULTRA

CULLODEN HOTEL

The Culloden is opposite the Ulster Folk and Transport Museum (a visit to the latter is a must). Drinks in the bar will be expensive, but for some it may be worth it, for the Gothic Room cocktail bar was once the private chapel (now deconsecrated) of the Bishop of Down. This excellent hotel was once the bishop's elegant Scots baronial mansion.

HILLSBOROUGH

HILLSIDE BAR

Food: Excellent pub grub

Hillsborough is an elegant suburb of Belfast. The local castle here is Queen Elizabeth's home away from home in Northern Ireland. While it might be amusing to ogle the castle, the thirsty visitor would do well to repair to the Hillside, whose deed is recorded in 1777, although the owner believes it to be older.

Unfortunately, I can find no better word to do the Hillside justice than the overworked "charming," but I can't help it—charming, it is. The bar is mahogany, of course, and there is a Guinness mirror, a tiny snug, and the best bar food this side of the Shannon. The pâté and the soups are homemade, and one can order such traditional Northern Irish fare as bread or biscuits with Augher cheddar cheese.

If you're not hungry, just sit by the open fire and sip. For lunchtime browsing, an attractive boutique and antique shop is also part of Hillside.

The Parting Glass

All the money e'er I had
I spent it in good company;
And all the harm I've ever done,
Alas! It was to none but me.
And all I've done for want of wit
To memory now I can't recall:
So fill to me the parting glass,
Good night and joy be with you all!

If I had money enough to spend
And leisure time to sit awhile,
There is a fair maid in this town
That sorely has my heart beguiled.
Her rosy cheeks and ruby lips
I own she has my heart in thrall
Then fill to me the parting glass
Good night and joy be with you all!

Oh, all the comrades e'er I had,
They're sorry for my going away;
And all the sweethearts I e'er had
They'd wish me one more day to stay,
But since it falls unto my lot
That I should rise and you should not,
I gently rise and softly call—
Good night and joy be with you all.

—Traditional ballad

INDEX

ACKNOWLEDGMENTS

Grateful acknowledgment is made for permission to reprint the following copyrighted material:
Excerpt from "The Irish Are Never Dull" by Marianne Baker from *Cosmopolitan* magazine, British edition, May 1978, reprinted by permission of *Cosmopolitan*.

Text of the pamphlet "Beezie's" reprinted by permission of Beezie's, Sligo, County Sligo.

Excerpts and the poem entitled "Phoenix Park" by Brendan Behan from *Brendan Behan's Island* (London: Hutchinson, 1962) reprinted by permission of Leresche and Sayle. Copyright © Brendan Behan, 1962.

Excerpt from "Patriot's Game" by Dominick Behan from *Ireland Sings* reprinted by permission of Westminster Music, Ltd.

Excerpt from "Ireland with Emily" by John Betjeman from *Collected Poems* reprinted by permission of John Murray (Publishers) Ltd.

Excerpt from an interview with Paul Brady in *In Dublin* magazine, No. 56 (July 1978), reprinted by permission of *In Dublin*.

Excerpt from "It's Been Copasthetic Here" by James Cameron from *The New Statesman*, August 5, 1966, reprinted by permission of *The New Statesman*.

"Ballydehob" by William Rossa Cole reprinted by permission of the author.

Excerpt from "The Valley of the Writers" by Frances Donnelley from *The Listener*, February 22, 1979, reprinted by permission of Frances Donnelley.

Excerpt from *Geo* magazine by Frances FitzGerald reprinted by permission of the author.

Excerpts from "The Long Memories of Mayo" by Thomas Flanagan from *Geo* magazine, April 1980, reprinted by permission of Wallace and Sheil Agency, Inc. Copyright © Thomas Flanagan, 1980.

Excerpt from *In Guilt and in Glory* by David Hanly reprinted by permission of William Morrow & Company, Inc., and Harold Matson Co., Inc. Copyright © David Hanly, 1979.

Excerpt from "Padraig O'Coanairre, Gaelic Story Teller" from *The Gap of Brightness* by F. R. Higgins reprinted by permission of Macmillan London and Basingstoke.

Excerpt from "Canal Bank Walk" by Patrick Kavanagh reprinted by permission of Katherine B. Kavanagh. Copyright © Katherine B. Kavanagh.

Excerpt from *All the Way to Bantry Bay* by Benedict Kiely reprinted by permission of the author and Victor Gollancz Ltd. Copyright © Benedict Kiely, 1978.

Descriptions of Sail Inn and Paddy's Pub in Tipperary courtesy of Hugh Leonard.

Excerpt from "Our Like Will Not Be There Again" by Lawrence Millman reprinted by permission of Little, Brown and Company.

Excerpt from *A Place Apart* by Dervla Murphy reprinted by permission of John Murray (Publishers) Ltd.

Excerpt from "Letters from the Great Blasket" by Eibhlís Ni Shúilleabháin reprinted by permission of The Mercier Press.

Excerpt from "Behan, Master of Language" by Flann O'Brien from *The Sunday Telegraph* (London), March 22, 1964, reprinted by permission of Brandt & Brandt Literary Agents, Inc. Copyright © the Estate of Flann O'Brien, 1964.

Excerpts from the pamphlet "The Bailey, The Story of a Famous Tavern" by Ulick O'Connor reprinted by permission of The Bailey.

Excerpt from *An Irish Journey* by Sean O'Faolain reprinted by permission of Curtis Brown, Ltd.

Excerpt from "Among the Irish" by V. S. Pritchett from *The New York Review of Books*, January 27, 1979, reprinted by permission of A. D. Peters and Company Ltd.

"Raftery the Poet" by Anthony Raftery, translated by Frank O'Connor, from *A Book of Ireland*, edited by Frank O'Connor, reprinted by permission of Fontana Books.

Excerpt from "The Public House Dynasts" by Ethna Ryan from *Business and Finance*, March 30, 1978, reprinted by permission of *Business and Finance*.

"Prelude" by J. M. Synge from *Poems and Translations* reprinted by permission of George Allen and Unwin (Publishers) Ltd.

Excerpt from "In West Kerry" by J. M. Synge from *Collected Works*, Vol. 2, reprinted by permission of Oxford University Press.

Epigraph reprinted by permission of Honor Tracy.

Excerpts from *Inside Ireland* reprinted by permission of Brenda Weir. Copyright © Inside Ireland Quarterly Newsletter and Information Service.

Excerpts from "The Double Vision of Michael Robartes," "The Lake Isle of Innisfree," *Collected Poems*, and *Autobiographies* by W. B. Yeats reprinted by permission of M. B. Yeats, Anne Yeats, Macmillan London Limited, and Macmillan Publishing Co., Inc., New York.